Exploring Creative Learning:
two primary schools and their partnerships

Edited by Catherine McGill, Teri N'Guessan
and Marion Rosen

Trentham Books
Stoke on Trent, UK and Sterling, USA

Trentham Books Limited
Westview House   22883 Quicksilver Drive
734 London Road   Sterling
Oakhill   VA 20166-2012
Stoke on Trent   USA
Staffordshire
England ST4 5NP

First published 2007

British Library Cataloguing-in-Publication Data
A catalogue record for this book is available from the British Library

ISBN-13: 978 1 85856 408 1

Designed and typeset by Trentham Print Design Ltd, Chester and printed in Great Britain by Cromwell Press Ltd, Trowbridge.

Contents

Acknowledgements • vi

Contributors • vii

Introduction • ix

Chapter 1
The structure of the project • 1
'What I want to know is: how is this going to work?'

Chapter 2
The impact on pupils • 23
'It's like doing it for yourself or breathing in your soul'

Chapter 3
Partnerships with arts organisations • 45
'I enjoyed it because I got to meet new people and
see what they could do'

Chapter 4
Partners' perspectives • 61
'I feel nervous because I'm going to have a new teacher
that I don't know well'

Chapter 5
Continuing professional development • 83
'I am developing the confidence to have a go'

Chapter 6
Assessing learning • 99
'Sometimes it's hard because you know what you enjoy but
you don't know what you've learnt – but actually you
have learnt something'

Chapter 7
Leadership • 119
Winning hearts and minds

Conclusion
A celebration of creative learning • 139

Glossary • 145

References • 149

Index • 151

Acknowledgements

Our thanks are first to the pupils and staff of Manor and Star Primary Schools whose hard work, commitment and forbearance made it possible for us to engage in the work described in this book. For most of us, it has been a rewarding journey – but never an easy one. We are also grateful to the parents and families of our pupils and to the governors of both schools for their support throughout the years. The names of children referred to in the text have been changed to maintain confidentiality.

Our thanks also to:

Andi Smith, Director of South West Newham EAZ, without whose support and encouragement this project would not have been possible

Peter Renshaw, our critical friend, who gave generously of his time reading and commenting on our writing

Martin Heaney and Pam Shaw, who travelled the journey with us as researchers

Matt Chappel, former deputy head at Star Primary, who stretched us intellectually

Vincent Marron and colleagues at the Keenan Institute in North Carolina who helped us to think more globally about creative learning

The Calouste Gulbenkian Foundation, for funding our early research

The Innovations Unit of the Department for Education and Skills, for funding further research

Creative Partnerships London East, that brokered and funded some of our partnerships with arts organisations.

Contributors

This book contains many contributions from children, parents, teachers, governors and others associated with the schools. Here we list only those who have written sections or whose interviews are quoted at length. Others are named in their contributions.

Petra Collins is a senior teacher and ICT leader at Manor Primary School.

Kate McGee is Deputy Head at Manor Primary School, with responsibility for assessment and teaching and learning.

Catherine McGill is an Advanced Skills Teacher, who works as a teacher-artist in Manor and Star Primary Schools. She undertook four years of research into children's views on their learning. She carried out most of the interviews with children, teachers, parents, and governors that are included in this book.

Judith Lathom-Kondell is a senior teacher and Literacy co-ordinator at Manor Primary.

Barbara Lo Guidice is a teacher at Manor Primary School with responsibility for mathematics.

Leesa Harbottle is a teacher and music co-ordinator at Star Primary School.

Donna Howard is the Nursery teacher at Star Primary School.

Martin Heaney is an independent researcher.

Christine Hudson is a teaching assistant at Star Primary School.

Stephen Mason is Education Officer at The Space. He was dancer in residence at Manor and Star Primary Schools in 2004 and 2005.

Teri N'Guessan is headteacher at Manor Primary School.

Violet Otieno is an Assistant Head at Star Primary School, with responsibility for teaching and learning.

Marion Rosen is headteacher at Star Primary School.

Andi Smith is Director of South West Newham EAZ and Principal Manager of Professional Development, Newham Children and Young Peoples Services.

Razia Sultana is a Nursery Nurse in the Nursery at Star Primary School.

Lucy Tingling is the Ethnic Minority Achievement co-ordinator at Star Primary School.

Amanda Wilson was the co-ordinator for Special Educational Needs at Star Primary School and now has responsibility for ICT.

Michelle Wilson is Assistant Head and arts co-ordinator at Manor Primary School.

Hannah Williams is currently a senior teacher at Manor Primary with responsibility for Special Educational Needs. Prior to that, she was art co-ordinator at Star Primary.

Lisle Von Buchenroder is Deputy Head at Star Primary School with responsibility for learning and teaching and assessment.

Introduction

Aims of the book

We are writing this now because the time is right. Since the publication of *Excellence and Enjoyment: A Strategy for Primary Schools* (2003) schools are being asked to work in more creative and collaborative ways. This book explores some of the issues and tensions involved in that process. It tracks our journey from entrenchment in the literacy and numeracy strategies and the Qualifications and Curriculum Authority (QCA) schemes of work to developing new ways of approaching teaching and learning.

We want to share our experiences with other practitioners – to tell the story and analyse the processes of our learning. This was a shared endeavour and we have invited everyone involved to put forward their views and reflect on their experiences. We have tried to capture all the voices: children, parents, staff, governors and external partners, as far as possible in their own words. As a result, you will find different, and occasionally conflicting, perspectives. We believe this is a strength, as it reflects the processes we have been through in the last five years and underlines the principle that diversity of viewpoints strengthens our schools as organisations. This is one of the themes that runs through the book and it is analysed in detail in Chapter 7. We have actively encouraged staff and pupils to question, challenge and engage with others in debate. This is part of the process of learning more about one's own views and beliefs for debate of this kind has played a major role in developing what many describe as a learning community.

Context

The schools that formed this creative learning partnership were Star Primary School, situated in Canning Town, and Manor Primary School in West Ham, East London. They are part of South West Newham Educational Action Zone which at that time had a brief to innovate in order to raise attainment. The

2001 census shows Newham has the most ethnically diverse population in Britain and is the fourth most disadvantaged borough in London and the eleventh in Britain, as judged by the Social Deprivation Index (2004). Both schools had a number of distinctive features:

- high teacher turnover and severe difficulties in staff recruitment, resulting in a lack of continuity and progression
- no culture of learning but a huge focus on behaviour management
- high number of incidents of challenging and disruptive pupil behaviour
- high rates of fixed and permanent exclusion
- large numbers of pupils on the special needs register with both behaviour and specific learning needs
- confrontational relationships with parents and carers
- low expectations and low aspirations
- low levels of attainment in the curriculum
- a high proportion of free school meals
- over 60% of pupils with English as an additional language, with over 50 languages spoken in each school
- a high percentage of children from refugee and asylum seeking families
- high pupil mobility and a largely transitional population
- a high proportion of social housing and private rentals in the area

The last five of the above are still features of the schools' profiles.

We embarked on this long-term partnership in the academic year 2001/02. The intention was to devise a model of curriculum reform that

- took account of theories of multiple intelligence
- focused on developing effective Continuing Professional Development (CPD) in the arts and an understanding of how they can enhance learning
- promoted strategies for involving the pupils in reflections on their experience
- promoted deep and lasting learning rather than shallow short term learning

Historically, this initiative followed two previous phases. They brought together artistic providers and teachers to develop strategies for engaging pupils in their learning and raising standards. They had been implemented in a number of schools but had involved limited numbers of staff and pupils. The emphasis had been on interpreting the existing curriculum rather than re-modelling. The principles were based on a model, A+ (Arts plus), developed in North Carolina, which explored the application of learning style theories and the arts to raise standards and levels of attainment.

These shorter-term projects indicated that engagement in the arts could affect pupil learning. Both phases had their successes but an evaluation recommended that a further research phase be introduced. It was suggested that this should involve two schools, working in close partnership, to develop new ways of interpreting or developing the curriculum and incorporating the arts into it. The emphasis on the arts caused a great deal of debate but ultimately we felt that, when taught well, the arts offered opportunities for the pupils to engage at an emotional level with learning and develop a whole range of cross-curricular skills and capacities including imagination, problem-solving, independence and confidence. All of which we felt were important to equip our pupils for the future.

The EAZ (Education Action Zone) appointed a teacher artist to support the work as part of a 2 year project.

The Gulbenkian Foundation and South West Newham EAZ funded the initial project. Without this the research element of the project would have been extremely difficult to maintain. Both schools made huge commitments in terms of time and money. In light of the research element and the creative focus of the work, Creative Partnerships London East offered the schools a role as associate partners and Newham Academy of Music asked us to pilot the Wider Opportunities programme.

Although the work done in previous phases had influenced teaching and learning in both schools, the emphasis on three learning styles: visual, auditory and kinaesthetic, led to a model that could potentially categorise pupils as particular types of learners. We wanted to look at learning more holistically and give pupils the opportunity to develop as many strategies as possible for learning. Our thinking was influenced by *All Our Futures*, Howard Gardner's theories of Multiple Intelligences, Golman's writing on Emotional Intelligence, theories on experiential learning, Philosophy for Children and brain-based research.

The labelling of the work we were doing as A+ and describing it as a project created problems. Some staff felt they were being asked to do something additional rather than develop their approaches to learning and teaching. We needed the label for funding and research purposes but it worked against curriculum reform. Eventually, after much debate, we decided that creative learning was a less restrictive label, one that encompassed the breadth of our intention and the open-ended nature of the work. So what began as A+ was re-labelled creative learning. We took our definition of creativity from *All Our Futures* (1999): 'Imaginative activity fashioned so as to produce outcomes that are both original and of value' (p29).

We do not have a definition of creative learning. We can describe it in terms of what we might see children, staff and leaders doing and what the school environment and climate is like. We have described some indicators in Chapter 6 but we do not claim to know enough to define it; we're still learning.

Although we have tried to use the term creative learning throughout this book there are times when it is necessary to refer to A+, particularly where process descriptions cover four years.

About the book
In this book we explore the tensions that exist between transmission models of teaching, and approaches that aim to lead to deeper learning for adults as well as children. Using the QCA schemes of work had led to a situation in our schools where teachers felt under pressure to deliver a great deal of content. We believe this is true in many primary schools. The values and purposes underlying the school curriculum and, indeed the National Curriculum, became lost, at least as far as English and Mathematics was concerned. It was a model based on transmission, as using schemes of work, whether QCA or others, assumes that a particular set of actions on the part of a teacher will result in particular learning on the part of pupils. Patently, this is not the case! However, the reality is that all our pupils are assessed using standardised tests – based on a transmission model – and we have a duty to help them to demonstrate their learning. This is largely at odds with the ways in which we work. Further tension exists in the pressure on schools to meet targets based on achievements in the tests. These are problems that we continue to struggle with and may never resolve in the current educational climate in Britain. Chapters 2 and 4 discuss these issues.

One of the principles underlying our work is the notion, as identified in the National Curriculum, of preparing children for an unknown future, where they may use technologies not yet invented; they may change jobs or professions several times in their lives. Our responsibility, then, is to equip children with the skills and understanding they need to be adaptable, solve problems, apply critical analysis and be flexible enough to engage fully in a future society. In our particular context, we felt an urgent need to address issues arising from the diversity of our immediate and wider community. Our starting point was a move away from a content-driven curriculum to one where there is a better balance between content, skills, learning habits and personal development – effectively returning to the original aims of the National Curriculum! Once this process started, it had an impact on every aspect of school life and led to whole school reform. This is not a simple model of change. It is an evolutionary process: as we started to change our approach to the curriculum, our thinking became more critical and we questioned our understanding of learning. This led to further changes, which in turn led us to more questioning and a yet deeper level of thinking. This has involved all the school community, through an on-going process of evaluation and discussion. To use current jargon, we are becoming a 'learning organisation'. We hope that this theme is obvious throughout the book.

Developing and maintaining a partnership, of whatever nature, can be a difficult and painful process but can bring great rewards through the synergy it generates. There were some who in various subtle ways resisted the notion of a long term partnership between the two schools, others who embraced it wholeheartedly. The tensions thus created have strengthened our schools as organisations because they forced us to analyse and reform our concept of leadership. They have also had an effect on the nature of professional discussions. These ideas are explored in Chapter 7 and are reflected in the range of voices that run throughout the book.

Partnerships with arts and other organisations pose a different set of challenges that arise through bringing together individuals with different perspectives on learning and education. Perhaps the most challenging issue for us has been in establishing these in a way that allows each partner to learn from the other. This is a change from the more traditional models of schools' involvement with arts organisations. Pre-planned, off the shelf packages and workshops are of little interest to us, as we look for partnerships that will have long term impact on children's learning and offer opportunities for staff to gain insights, understanding and skills. In Chapters 3 and 4 teachers and artists describe the ways in which this works for us. How this supports children's and adults' learning and how it has changed our approaches to teaching is described in Chapters 2 and 5 and is another theme running throughout the book.

1
THE STRUCTURE OF THE PROJECT
'What I want to know is: how is this going to work?'

his is what we were asked by a boy in Year 6. We begin our answer with
teacher-artist Catherine McGill's account of the structure of the
schools partnership and the processes employed to develop the curriculum, establish new partnerships and explore a new model of Continuing
Professional Development. The director of the Education Action Zone, staff,
pupils and parents from across both the schools add their views.

In the beginning... *Catherine McGill*

I had been working at one of the schools before I became the teacher-artist
across both schools. I had been teaching in primary schools for ten years but
my passion had always been for teaching visual arts. I strongly believed that
experience of working in the arts was essential for all round pupil development. From personal experience, I also knew it could make the difference between engagement in learning or not. I am also a practising artist and have
some understanding of the thought processes involved in creating art.

The schools that formed this creative learning partnership were Star Primary
School, situated in Canning Town, and Manor Primary School in West Ham,
East London. They are part of South West Newham Educational Action Zone
which at that time had a brief to innovate in order to raise attainment. The
2001 census shows Newham has the most ethnically diverse population in
Britain and is the fourth most disadvantaged borough in London and the
eleventh in Britain, as judged by the Social Deprivation Index (2004). Both
schools had a number of distinctive features: high number of incidents of
challenging and disruptive pupil behaviour; high rates of fixed and permanent exclusion; large numbers of pupils on the special needs register; low

expectations and low aspirations; low levels of attainment in the curriculum; high proportion of free school meals; over 60% of pupils with English as an additional language, with over 50 languages spoken in each school; a high percentage of children from refugee and asylum seeking families; high pupil mobility; a high proportion of social housing and private rentals in the area.

When we embarked on this project we really had very little idea about where we were going and how we would get there.

Two groups were established – a steering group and an operational group. The steering group initially included researchers and local authority personnel as well as head teachers, deputies and myself. Their role was to suggest, discuss and advise on possible ways forward both in terms of research and structure. The operational group consisted of arts co-ordinators, deputies, the director of the EAZ and headteachers. This second group considered how changes might be managed within each school, and what might be necessary to implement them. We later established another group, the Creative Learning Team, made up of staff, teachers, teaching assistants and learning mentors, from across the schools. That group enabled us to discuss ideas and their impact and get feedback from a range of perspectives. Over time the makeup of these groups shifted. After four years the steering group was no longer relevant and the operational group and the creative learning team now maintain the partnership and identify future developments.

Initially we agreed that we needed to

■ approach the project with open minds and give staff licence to try out new ideas, create a culture of learning which valued learning from 'mistakes'

Andi, Director SW Newham EAZ

The initial discussions with the steering group were profound. Like throwing a stone into a lake, they had a ripple effect on how both schools created infrastructures to ensure that there was strategic direction and operational processes. Then they set up the creative learning team and the teacher/ research group. The creative learning team in particular provides a route through which everyone can engage in debates on learning whether it's at an operational or strategic level. This is important because it gives ownership and it gets a groundswell of contributions from everybody. I think this infrastructure has been organically created because it has grown out of purpose; in the same way as pupils have a voice, it enables the school workforce to have a voice and a forum for discussion.

- evaluate the process continually and respond to challenges identified

- give staff opportunities to develop their own knowledge and understanding of the arts, both in and outside the classroom

- inform and refine our own understanding of how the arts support children's learning

and that my role in particular would include

- facilitating researchers so they gained access to both statistical data and individuals in the schools.

- working collaboratively with each year group in both schools to develop units of work that linked curriculum areas with the arts

- identifying how those units linked to the National Curriculum and the multiple intelligences suggested by Howard Gardner

- providing workshops for staff to develop skills, knowledge and understanding related to the art activities involved in the units developed

- talking with children before and after units to establish their views on their experience

A daunting task!

The schools had had little contact before so we tried to introduce the project to the staff in a way that would serve several purposes. We agreed to hold two days of training in July 2002, to prepare for the changes in September. There would be theoretical and practical sessions for teachers and support staff and the chance for people to get to know each other.

Around 120 staff were involved, quite a large number of people to work with. Feedback from staff varied but generally their feelings ranged from excitement to trepidation, and some expressed resistance to change. I think that some of those who had been in the profession for a while thought that what

---

Donna, teacher

I'll be perfectly honest – when the A+ project first started I thought this is something else we have got to do. I think we all felt like that. We felt we were very creative anyway in the nursery. I suppose it was me, because I find it hard to change. I like to get new ideas but you think 'well what are they going to teach us?' but when we got into it I thought it was really good. I have really enjoyed all the projects we have done.

> *Andi, Director SW Newham EAZ*
>
> The first two day programme aimed to
>
> - set the ethos for creative learning
> - provide pragmatic and conceptual mapping of creative learning work to school-based initiatives
> - provide art form and skills based workshops
> - explore pedagogical studies of learning
> - set the framework for Action Research methodology
> - explore practical methods for incorporating research into planning and vice versa
> - convey the importance of communication, critical reflection, information, evaluation
> - explain the role of the teacher–artist within the schools
> - describe specific planning methods
> - explore strategies for good practice
> - discuss dissemination of effective practice
> - describe continuing professional development

we planned to do was to return pre-National Curriculum topic teaching. There were also understandable concerns about whether or not the work would raise achievement in the core subjects. The debate about improving levels of attainment still continues.

The active workshops the staff took part in were designed to help develop their expertise in the arts and their understanding of the learning process.

> *Christine, teaching assistant, reflecting on initial INSET*
>
> When it first started I didn't know where it was going, what it was really about. It was thoroughly enjoyable, I did enjoy it and it really stuck in my mind. We had a story line and we had to mime it... when you first started it was quite embarrassing...
>
> *Linda, teaching assistant*
>
> I think there was a sort of Star and Manor divide in the beginning, it wasn't intentional. I think it is because we are such a big staff here we may have seemed intimidating... I don't think it was anybody's fault.

Barbara, Teacher

As a newly qualified teacher I took this challenge on board with immense enthusiasm and open mindedness, which I believe, are key elements for projects such as this to succeed. The fact that I was relatively inexperienced in teaching probably helped my approach to the challenges that were placed on us. One of the most challenging aspects of the project was jumping into the void. I had never experienced or experimented with this approach to teaching and learning and in some ways we were left to develop ideas that were quite unrefined, in any way we thought appropriate. On one hand it terrified me to have so few boundaries and little guidance but on the other hand I was excited by the prospect of trying out a new approach and perhaps knowing that people had enough faith in me to encourage me to do so.

What was probably the hardest task for me was to let go of complete control over the children's learning and begin to let them choose where they wanted to take their learning.

My first project was a geography and dance combined exploration of different environments with a year 1 class. The idea was to explore a variety of environments such as a busy city, the sky, the sea and a forest through the medium of dance.

Having no pre-conceived ideas of the outcomes or processes, I could listen to the voices of the children with a genuinely open mind and was willing to follow their suggestions about what we could explore next. We explored the local environment through photography and drawing. The children made informed choices of media and subjects. Gradually they took control of their learning, with me merely acting as facilitator and, I'm hoping, as inspiration.

The power of choice

Having been given more control over my teaching, I was able to think more creatively and to experiment with processes and media that I would have previously have considered risky. Soon after my first project, I started using physical education and dance as media for teaching literacy. It proved very successful; the children responded enthusiastically and enjoyed the new experience.

Most importantly it has given me greater confidence to venture into the unknown without being afraid of failure. I somehow managed to rid myself of the constraints that I felt needed to be in place for me as a teacher, to ensure effective teaching.

The most significant impact though has been on the children. Not knowing where the learning will take you, frightening and unsettling as it is for a teacher, is liberating for the children. Not having pre-conceived outcomes and focusing on the processes eliminates for the children the fear of not complying with the teacher's expectations. A child who has no fear of failing will flourish and develop creativity and imagination.

Some of the feedback from group discussion about the project proposal appear opposite.

We gave the teachers time to work with the teachers of their parallel year group in the other school, to identify curriculum areas and art forms they wanted to create a unit from for the following year. There was much debate about the concept of creativity and what it meant. For planning purposes we adopted the definition in *All our Futures* (1999): 'Imaginative activity fashioned so as to produce outcomes that are both of original and of value' p29.

We returned to that debate repeatedly over the years because although the arts can be powerful in engaging pupils in learning, creativity does not lie solely within the realm of the arts.

The new creative learning units

In the first year I worked with each year group from both schools, developing, planning and evaluating units of work on subjects identified by the staff. I then worked alongside the teachers, sometimes modelling lessons where requested and sometimes team-teaching, in all but one year group. Some of the units were more successful than others, but it seemed that the greater the challenges the greater the learning for everyone concerned. Initially, I think one of the problems was that we were sometimes over ambitious and tried to include too much curriculum content and too many art forms.

During the first year internal evaluation indicated that to develop understanding and specific skills everyone involved, including the support staff, had to attend planning meetings and workshops. For example, Year 4 staff wanted to develop a unit that linked religious concepts to textile work and this meant thinking about how ideas can be visually represented. Once we established the process the pupils would go through we realised that the staff would need to experience that process themselves. They all had different experiences of working with textiles and with religious concepts and the workshop gave them the confidence to work on the theme with their pupils. But there were times when it was impossible to organise cover for all those concerned.

> *Teaching assistant*
>
> This year the support staff were not involved in the planning so we had no input. The workshops we did take part in were useful but we did not feel we had a chance to revisit them or use them.

Feedback from staff about project proposals after initial Inset

What it might offer pupils

- opportunities to communicate more
- increased self-esteem
- increased concentration
- opportunities to develop personal interests
- increased motivation and enthusiasm
- a wider range of opportunities for achievement
- greater choice
- increased accessibility for pupils with English as an additional Language
- a culturally inclusive curriculum
- encourages self expression
- develops collaborative skills
- utilises the energy of physical learners
- brings excitement back into school

Possible issues

- implications for assessment
- ensuring continuity and progression
- relevance to pupils' lives and value systems
- resources and funding
- whether the structure and organisation of the schools could be flexible enough to encourage and promote more creative teaching
- the distinction between the arts achievement and academic achievement might create a problem

Questions

- What about children who don't like the arts?
- What will society need in the future?
- Haven't good teachers been doing this for years?
- What about Information and Communication Technology?
- Are the ways of thinking developed in the arts transferable?
- Is it sustainable?

After the first unit was completed some teachers and teaching assistants began to incorporate some of the strategies and principles of the units into their everyday teaching.

When we asked the staff at the end of the first year what they wanted to develop in the following year, they mentioned two areas which we felt we lacked the expertise to support well: dance and puppetry. Partly through the brokerage and funding from Creative Partnerships, and partly through school funds, we were able to address both those issues. The schools employed a dancer, Stephen Mason, for one term to work with Year 3 and 6 and we negotiated a programme for Nursery and Year 2 with the Little Angel Puppet Theatre.

Although I had worked in partnership with other artists in schools, working across two schools and managing the complexities of timetables, planning and expectations was challenging. So this was another steep learning curve.

The residency with Stephen was so successful that the following year we managed to employ him for the whole year to work with every year group. So in the third year most year groups developed two units, one of them dance-related. In Foundation Stage and Key Stage 1 Stephen worked with a composer and in Key Stage 2 he worked alongside another dancer. For some of the units Stephen refined his previous work which the teachers wanted to be

Barbara, class teacher

The idea of embarking on a journey of discovery with your class has been for me one of the foundations of this project. The skills, knowledge and understanding that would be acquired on the way and the outcome was unknown, but it didn't matter. What was fundamental for me was the journey, the choices, ensuring the children discovered their own voices unfettered by teachers' expectations.

What is happening now however is that the projects are repeated each year as well as developed further but with each repetition we are in danger of losing the spontaneity, the enthusiasm perhaps, and the essence of why we started our creative learning partnership in the first place. I fear that creative learning may be regarded merely as another 'box' which future generations will strive to think outside.

If you repeat a project already explored and effectively created by other pupils, however hard the teacher and the class may try to make it their own, outcomes and expectations may loom over the children. Teachers will look at previous years' artifacts and expect their children to achieve similar results. This will affect their classroom practice, expectations will be set and the children's voices may be suffocated.

Early Years staff

The workshops and planning have been very useful and it has been essential that all staff have been included. We feel confident to contribute to planning and implementing projects.

developed further. The table on pages 10-13 identifies the units that were developed as a partnership rather than some of the unintentional outcomes that arose from the work. Many teachers and year groups changed their ways of working in other areas of the curriculum in the light of what they learned from the partnership work.

In the fourth year we decided not to insist that a new unit be developed but to have the year groups concentrate on consolidation. To continue fostering

Year 3 pupils discussing learning journals

The units developed in the first three years

	2002/3	2003/4	2004/5	2004/5 dance project
Nursery	**Nursery Outcomes** Explore clay and create a representation of something that is special to the pupils **Related Early Years Goals** Knowledge and Understanding of the World Personal and Social Development Communication, Language and Literacy Creative Development	**Outcomes** Explore various methods of combing and joining materials to make puppets. **Related Early Years Goals** Knowledge and Understanding of the World Personal and Social Development Communication, Language and Literacy Creative Development	**Outcomes** Nursery chose to develop further a previous unit	**Outcomes** The opportunity to participate and enjoy dance and music activities related to story **Related Early Years Goals** Knowledge and Understanding of the World Personal and Social Development Communication, Language and Literacy Creative Development Physical Development
Reception	**Reception Outcomes** Explore various methods of combing and joining materials to make puppets. **Related Early Years Goals** ■ Knowledge and Understanding of the World ■ Personal and Social Development ■ Communication, Language and Literacy ■ Creative Development	**Outcomes** Use a book as a starting point for exploring characters and settings through music dance and drama **Related Early Years Goals** ■ Knowledge and understanding of the world ■ Personal and Social Development ■ Communication, Language and Literacy ■ Creative Development	**Outcomes** Develop knowledge and understanding of materials and create special objects which have significance for them **Related Early Years Goals** ■ Knowledge and understanding of the world ■ Personal and Social Development ■ Communication, Language and Literacy ■ Creative Development ■ Mathematical Development	**Outcomes** Use a story as the starting point to explore how the characteristics of animals can be conveyed through movement and music **Related Early Years Goals** ■ Knowledge and understanding of the world ■ Communication, Language and Literacy ■ Creative Development ■ Physical Development

2000/3

Y1 Outcomes

Explore the differences in environments through music and dance.

Related curriculum areas

- Literacy
- Music
- Dance

Y2 Outcomes

Explore emotions and how they can be recognised and represented through dance, music and art

Related curriculum areas

- Personal, Health, Social, Citizenship, Education
- Dance
- Music
- Art
- Literacy

2003/4

Outcomes

Explore the subject of themselves and represent several different aspects of themselves visually and through collage

Related curriculum areas

- Art
- Personal, Health, Social, Citizenship Education
- Science
- Religious Education

Outcomes

Combine and join a variety of materials to represent a character of the pupils making and collaboratively construct a story using that character

Related curriculum areas

- Design and Technology
- Literacy
- Art

2004/5

Outcomes

Explore how to create movement in images and toys related to stories and films and produce an artefact

Related curriculum areas

- Design and Technology
- Literacy
- Art

Outcomes

Visit a number of sites and consider the structure and purpose of bridges. Use a variety of materials to construct their own bridges

Related curriculum areas

- Geography
- Design and Technology
- Art

2004/5 dance project

Outcomes

Use books as the starting point for exploring different kinds of environments

Related curriculum areas

- Literacy
- Dance
- Music

Outcomes

Develop pupils' knowledge and understanding of emotions and how they can be conveyed through body language, movement and music

Related curriculum areas

- Personal, Health, Social, Citizenship Education
- Music
- Dance
- Literacy

2002/3

Y3 Outcomes

Explore the pupils local environment, identify changes over time and gather visual resources before selecting and refining a composition and creating a series of reliefs.

Related curriculum areas

■ Geography

■ Art

Y4 Outcomes

Develop knowledge and understanding of religions represented in the local area, consider the pupils' beliefs and understandings in key life events. Develop a symbol which reflect their own beliefs, in textiles, and create poems.

Related curriculum areas

■ Religious Education Philosophy for Children

■ Art

■ Literacy

2003/4

Outcomes

Explore concepts related to magnets and springs through dance

Related curriculum areas

■ Science

■ Dance

Outcomes

Develop their understanding of environments and plant life through a variety of visits, collect visual information. Explore the use of organic forms to create patterns before constructing a living sculpture.

Related curriculum areas

■ Science

■ Geography

■ Art

2004/5

Outcomes

Develop observational drawing skills in relation to a particular curriculum area and engage in two print processes

Related curriculum areas

■ Art,

■ Personal, Health, Social, Citizenship Education

■ Religious Education

Outcomes

Develop their understanding of the impact of diet on health. Explore a variety of photographic processes and use photography and ICT to produce a poster related to healthy eating.

Related curriculum areas

■ Personal, Health, Social, Citizenship Education

■ Information and Communication Technology

■ Literacy

2004/5 dance project

Outcomes

Explore scientific concepts related to magnets and springs through dance

Related curriculum areas

■ Science

■ Dance

Outcomes

Use movement to explore geographical features and the differences and similarities between two places

Related curriculum areas

■ Geography

■ Dance

■ Philosophy for Children

2002/3

Y5 Outcomes

Develop an understanding of the effects of Tudor exploration and present their understanding in a variety of ways

Related curriculum areas

- History
- Maths
- Literacy
- Drama
- Art

Y6 Outcomes

Analyse and consider issues around the environment. Explore various film techniques before producing a short film with an environmental message.

Related curriculum areas

- Geography
- Literacy
- Art
- Information and Communication Technology

2003/4

Outcomes

Develop an understanding of how sound is produced and how it can be changed. Design and make an instrument of the pupil's own invention. Collaboratively compose and play a piece of music on their instrument

Related curriculum areas

- Science
- Music
- Design and Technology

Outcomes

Explore a number of scientific concepts through dance.

Related curriculum areas

- Dance
- Science

2004/5

Outcomes

Explore, through visits and ICT, land use in East London and how that has changed over time. Select an area and period of time to represent in textiles

Related curriculum areas

- Information and Communication Technology
- Geography
- Design and Technology

Outcomes

Develop specific musical knowledge and understanding and their relationship to mathematical concepts

Related curriculum areas

- Maths
- Music

2004/5 dance project

Outcomes

Explore issues around bullying through dance

Related curriculum areas

- Personal, Health, Social, Citizenship Education,
- Dance
- Literacy

Outcomes

Explore a number of environmental issues through dance and articulate their own opinions about them

Related curriculum areas

- Geography
- Dance
- Personal, Health, Social, Citizenship Education

the discussion and skills development which had helped move on their think-ing, each year group was asked to identify

- an area where they wanted to plan together
- the focus for a practical workshop
- a time at which they would share some work they had done across the two schools

They were also asked to say whether they wanted me to work alongside them at any point and what I might do. Most often they wanted to involve me when they were tackling a unit of which they had little experience, because they had changed year groups, or where their experience had prompted them to con-sider making certain changes.

One of the issues that has arisen over the last four years and continues to be of concern is how to keep the creative learning units fresh. As they move up the school, each year will present pupils with new challenges which, we hope, will build on previous experience. But we recognise that teachers may come to look upon the creative units as just another programme of study. This can only be avoided if the teachers themselves consider previous evaluations and how they might change a plan to give more ownership to both their current group of children and themselves. We have tried to encourage teachers to look at the processes involved rather than the outcomes.

Conversation with parents about pupils sharing learning across the schools

Laura – I don't think it's negative, they learn to mix with other schools as well. Where they are always going to Star and Star coming here they learn to mix. It pre-pares them for leaving really because they are not going to go with all their class when they leave.

Anne Marie – They do get on very well when they get together. They know a few of their names and they say ' oh we're going to see so-and -so this one when we go to Star today,' so they're making friends. Which is good really. There's loads of rivalry in the secondary schools isn't there. It's a good idea to get it out of the way before they go up to secondary. Sometimes they say 'Star this and that 'or 'they're our enemies' and you can't be like that can you?

Donna – There's no negative things really. The only thing I noticed is when they did that concert down at the tabernacle, it was Star, Manor and another school, we only had a handful of kids and Star had masses of them.

When we were in [the other school] there were about three groups dancing at a time and then three groups watching and there were like a hundred kids watching you so it's really like embarrassing. *Year 4 pupil*

Sharing the work

We had agreed that we would arrange a meeting between the children from every year group in both schools at the end of each unit so they could see each other's work and discuss their learning. Logistically this was tricky because we had to find a way of facilitating discussions between 150 pupils. As one school was a three form and the other a two form entry, the pupils of the smaller school sometimes felt overwhelmed and defensive. It took us quite a while to find strategies to overcome this.

Year 3 pupils discussing printing processes

In some cases, the notion of sharing led to greater emphasis being placed on the outcome or product than the process. This was partly due to an element of competition between the schools and partly to the scrutiny of outsiders, including the researchers. For example, in the first year when one year group worked on environments and movement and performed their work to each other, knowing that this was going to happen influenced the processes the pupils went through and the emphasis became fixed on outcome.

Eventually we got better at finding ways of sharing work across the schools so that more emphasis was placed on process.

As the use of learning journals developed, we found we could use them as a starting point for the pupils discussions. We found that if we split the pupils sharing their dance into small groups and structured it as a dance lesson, everybody felt more relaxed and enjoyed it more.

Sometimes alternative venues were used for the shared sessions. For example one Year 3 group had been doing some work on the local built environment. After they had explored through drawing, they created relief sculptures and castings. Then they took their sketchbooks and some of their work to a nearby open space, where we laid it out so the children could look at and discuss one another's work.

Although some pupils showed some resistance to sharing, on the whole it was beneficial. Sharing allowed the pupils to see a wider range of outcomes from the same processes. They saw that their school world was not unique and that other schools might have different things to offer or might approach things in different ways.

Continuing Professional Development

The arts experience across the staff of the schools varied enormously. Some had extensive knowledge and understanding of a particular art form; others had little experience of any. We carried out a needs analysis, asking them to identify their perceived strengths and weaknesses. We repeated this several times over the four years and used the information to make decisions about training and development sessions as well as arts partnerships.

We also used the strengths of the staff to provide some of the training sessions, thereby extending their own expertise. Feedback from staff in the earlier sessions suggested that although this was fairly successful we needed to think more carefully about differentiation. Despite trying hard to differentiate there are still times when we receive feedback that suggests we don't always get it right.

Kate, teacher

I had a lot of experience of teaching the arts in the curriculum but I tended to do it discretely rather than in combination with other curriculum areas. I thought instinctively that the arts were a good way of engaging pupils and I was looking forward to being able to implement that in a more structured way.

Faye, Teacher

I didn't have a clue about the arts. I was educated in South Africa. The problem with education in South Africa is that if you were white you were quite privileged; you would have an art room and music and all the teachers and equipment. If you were classed as coloured you didn't have that advantage, PE was basically run around the school, long distance, or you would do aerobics. Art was non-existent because we had nothing. For music we had no instruments so basically it was non-existent.

In my first year of training we did some art, some PE and a bit of music and then we had to choose. I did PE for my second year and then in my third and fourth I did no creative subjects at all. It was purely academic, but you could choose.

I would say that over the last four years my confidence has grown immensely. I think if you said to me now I need to do a dance lesson, I would be quite happy to do that – in any of the arts really, although obviously I would feel more confident in some than in others. My confidence has grown because of the opportunities for development that have been offered.

The child's voice

Pupils were frequently invited to reflect on the processes they were engaged in and the ensuing discussions often informed their next steps. Before they took part in a unit, I interviewed groups of pupils about what they thought they knew already and then at the end of it I talked with them about what had gone well, what they had learned and if they had improvements to suggest. Pupils also completed questionnaires about a specific unit. The feedback was then used alongside teacher evaluation to consider adaptations for the next group of pupils.

Andi, Director SW Newham EAZ

When you are putting together any project plan you have some desired outcomes and they would be raised attainment, improved communications between the two schools and improved levels of arts skills. The outcomes exceeded our expectations and resulted in whole school transformation in both schools. They undertook a process of self-review as learning organisations and this led to their use of Continuing Professional Development in a differentiated way. I feel that the project itself has helped us to understand the need for differentiated professional learning.

> We only had about half an hour or an hour to do bits of it and that wasn't enough. *Year 5 pupil*
>
> Maybe next year you could have two (printing presses) for each group because we were all squashed. *Year 4 pupil*
>
> When we were looking at our pictures and thinking about what to write we didn't get that much time so we didn't get to write too many things and not that many ideas are in it but I think we should have more time so that we can get more ideas. *Year 4 pupil*

At the beginning of the project (Autumn 2002) I worked with Matt Chapel, then Deputy of Star Primary, to devise a questionnaire that would give us an overall picture of pupils' ideas about the curriculum. We considered what a good learner would be like and then devised questions which would give us information on which to base our plan for learning and to evaluate the impact of the work we had done. The questions gave us information about the pupils'

- attitudes to different curriculum areas including the arts
- the learning strategies they used
- ideas about how they thought working in the arts might be useful to them

The questionnaire was completed in September 2002 and subsequently in July of 2003, 2004, 2005, 2006. The pupils answered closed questions but also had opportunities for reflection and a more considered written response. I collated the yes/no responses and we used them to consider possible developments that would benefit the pupils.

For example, 80% of pupils who completed the first questionnaire identified painting as something they enjoyed. It was by far the highest positive

> Pupil 1 – It lasted very long and it seemed like it was going, not forever, but for quite long, and we was going over the same thing. Everyone was finished and we was practicing and practicing and that was a cool thing but then it went on and people started to get a bit bored
>
> Pupil 2 – I don't agree with that, cause I think we should have had longer so we could have more practice. Some people were like me; I had to go to a thing (group lesson) during that so I didn't get much practice

Lisle, Deputy Head

The maze project was very successful. There was a great feel good factor which came out of it. People really got involved and were beginning to understand the theory behind what we were trying to do in relation to creativity.

response. So we decided that we would design a project that would give every child an opportunity to paint. And consultation with the pupils in both schools had identified their interest in improving their playground. We devised a plan that would respond to both concerns: the maze project.

We identified a different theme for each year group and each class worked on researching and exploring ideas around their theme before collaboratively creating designs to paint onto large boards. The painted boards were fixed to the playground floor to provide quiet areas or just to create visual impact. The pupils were delighted with the work. They visited each other's schools and looked at each other's work. Each child received a postcard with images of the maze boards, on which they could write an evaluative comment.

Maze boards in situ

Key skills

During the first term there was a good deal of debate about maintaining rigour in teaching and learning. We wanted to find a way of structuring pupils' learning that crossed the curriculum boundaries. The end result of this was that we identified four key cross-curricular skills that we considered essential in both the development of effective learners and in good arts practice. The four we initially selected were

- evaluation
- making links
- meta learning
- questioning

We refer to these as our key skills, rather than the National Curriculum key skills.

Interview, Petra, class teacher

Going back to key skills I remembered why I wanted to become a teacher. It helps me to think about individuals and realise that knowing the order of Henry VIII's wives is not going to help the pupils at any stage of their lives, but that knowing how to find that out, understanding its impact on British history or just forming your own opinion about what they think about him is more important. They may not have all the facts but I know if I asked them to find something out they would be able to, because I have concentrated on that key skill.

I did an independent learning project on the Olympics last year. I decided to let them find it out for themselves. I thought I had gone a long way towards giving the children more autonomy. However I realised that I still find it difficult to know that at the end of six weeks they will not necessarily all be able to do what I want them to do or know what I want them to know. They loved it; they were allowed to present what they had learnt in any way they thought appropriate. That was hard because we had plays that weren't relevant, posters that missed useful information or relevant ideas. I had to accept that if I was giving the children ownership then that is what would happen. They were deciding what was relevant and that might have been different to my view of what was relevant. We could evaluate what we were doing but if they could justify it I would have been wrong to say no. The only way they will get better will be to keep giving them that freedom and to keep helping them to think through what they are doing... what they get out of the process is far more important than the content.

The key skills are important. They help you remember and gain a better perspective about what and why you are teaching. You can become bogged down in teaching to tests and expecting children to have certain knowledge rather than skills and valuing regurgitation rather than understanding. If you leave it to them you know what they understand and how to help them move on from where they are.

Interview, Donna, Nursery teacher

The way we use the key skills in our planning has worked out quite well. We did start off changing them each week and that was too much because there are so many children in here and we couldn't make sure all the children covered all of them. So we changed it so that every half term we focus on one key skill from each box and that works a lot better. When we are working on focused activities we have the learning objective and the key skill in mind and we are making mental notes of things like 'he is evaluating his work' or 'he's very proud of what he has done'. Then we make notes in their profiles. And sometimes we look through and we find there is a key skill that wasn't met so we might keep it on for the next half term and see where we could do things differently. I think it has changed the way we work. They don't know they are evaluating, but we can see them doing it.

Once we had identified these broad categories, the staff across the schools worked in year groups to develop a progression map with descriptions of expectations from Nursery to Year 6. Statements drawn from that map were tied to the unit overviews and individual session plans.

During the third year, after discussion, we added two more skills:

- personal communication
- purposeful problem solving (as opposed to solving puzzles)

We recognised, as did the pupils, that many of the units that had been developed presented good opportunities for both collaborative work and problem solving. In the process of working collaboratively pupils needed to be able to express their own ideas, respond to the ideas of others and negotiate ways forward. It seemed a logical point to look more carefully at those two skills and build them into the progression map already established for the other four key skills.

Over the years we have refined and developed our understanding of the key skills we identified and also the way we use them across the curriculum. Children automatically evaluate both their learning and the processes of learning, they use questioning to extend their understanding and they make links between their learning in different situations and subjects.

Conclusion

This chapter describes the structures we developed to enable the project to happen. It discusses the role of the teacher-artist as a facilitator, and some of the changes that were needed in order to provide a framework that would support all staff in clarifying and developing their thinking about learning in the broadest context.

The changes that occurred during the initial period of the project were a direct result of continuous evaluation and the identification of structures that would support, rather than hinder, the move towards a more creative and engaging curriculum.

2

THE IMPACT ON PUPILS
'It's like doing it for yourself or breathing in your soul' Year 4 pupil

This chapter focuses on the effect of the Project on the pupils. There is an interview with a class teacher, Petra Collins, about her first experience of a new unit of work. Alongside, Judith Lathom-Kondell, a parallel class teacher, describes her views of the same unit. Amanda Wilson, Special Needs co-ordinator, describes the observed impacts of creative learning on some children who have special needs. There is also an extract from a paper, by Catherine McGill, teacher-artist, which explored what the pupils felt they could learn from the arts.

Interview with Petra

Judith and I had taught the Year 4 curriculum the previous year (2001/2) and we found a QCA scheme of work called 'Religions in our Neighborhood' very vague. It relied on data collection and enquiry skills. We were both observed during an Ofsted inspection in October 2001 and the inspectors agreed with us that the children had no knowledge of local religions, that they confused race and religion and were neither interested nor motivated by religion. This surprised me because I had previously found children to be very interested in people's beliefs. However, it was such a bland scheme that didn't seem to have much purpose; it didn't connect with the children or with us. So when we had the planning session with the Star teachers, that was the first thing Judith and I suggested. The Star teachers had also found the scheme hard to teach, so we agreed it would be the perfect thing to inject some creativity into and that we could use art to bring it to life.

I can't remember how it happened, but we all settled on the idea of textiles. Then we all decided at some point in the planning process to fix on certain

> *Judith – teacher*
>
> In 2001/2 I was based in Year 4 for the first time and was getting to grips with some of the topics covered in that year group. The Geography topic of India and the RE topic of Religions in our Neighbourhood presented the most demanding problems. The first problem was that the school lacked resources in these areas and secondly, I was not aware of the religions in the local community. After teaching these subjects as stand alone subjects, my year partner, Petra, and I decided that we had to find a way of integrating the topics to make them more relevant to the children the following year. As the three main religions we were focusing on were all practised in India, we decided we would introduce an India week as this would give us the scope to explore different aspects of the country. We agreed that the children would complete a mini-project on some aspect of India, e.g. the food, the industry etc and that we would visit a mandir (Hindu temple) a church and a mosque in the local area to give the children an insight into these three major religions practised in India.

ceremonies rather than try and learn everything about all religions. The pupils lacked knowledge and experience of world religions so we decided to focus on births, marriages and deaths. What transpired was a real experience for the children and for us. It turned into one of the best pieces of work I think I have ever done.

We had combined RE concepts with real self-expression through art and poetry writing in literacy. The children excelled in all three. We used lots of different strategies for them to learn about the religions and how birth, marriage and death are marked in them. We decided we wanted them to have visits so we went to lots of places of worship. We interviewed adults and children, from our own and other classes both younger and older, so it really was about the local community. We researched on the Internet and looked at books, but it really was the visits to places of worship and the interviews that had the biggest impact and made it real to the children. The previous year we had only used secondary sources.

From there, the children wanted to think about their own views. Views is the wrong word – I suppose it was their own spirituality and morals about birth,

> *Year 4 boys*
>
> I liked doing it (the poem) I liked saying the poem and doing the actions.
>
> I enjoyed the poems because the poems just made it more exciting.

Judith – teacher

The creative learning partnership, created at the end of the summer term 2002, gave us an opportunity to take our ideas a lot further without feeling the constraints of the National Curriculum. In consultation with the Year 4 teachers from Star Primary we devised a scheme of work for a half term that made links between Literacy, Religious Education and Art.

The aim of this unit was for the children to explore the ideas of birth, death and marriage and create their own poetry and an abstract symbol that reflected their own ideas.

At Manor School we decided to proceed with the India Week in order to build the children's interest. We organised parents to come in to talk about their experiences of living in the North or South of India and how this affected their diet, style of dress and their appearance. As a bonus they also cooked some Indian food and brought it in for the children to sample. The children used books and the Internet to research aspects of India.

We had a trip to our local mandir, where food was again provided for the children to sample as part of the experience. The children were told about the religion and allowed to ask questions about how birth, marriage and death were regarded and how they were celebrated. The trips to a local church and mosque, arranged with the help of the Imam who ran the after school Arabic class, followed and the children explored these religions in some depth.

---

marriage and death. We hadn't specifically planned for that and afterwards I realised it was exactly what we should have been planning for in Religious Education.

Although I had done projects before in the school, the children had a fixed idea about art being drawing and painting and looking like something. We decided to use symbolism in religions to put across the idea of a symbol being something more abstract, having meaning but not necessarily looking like something. It took a great deal of work. We hadn't expected the children to struggle so much with the notion of symbolism. I think because it was such a struggle, it was such a big thing when they did get there that the sense of achievement was huge and that had a knock on effect throughout the year. They didn't just grasp the concept in relation to that unit, they understood that not all art had to be representational and they began to develop an understanding of art and poetry as self-expression. Primary school art tends to be more about assimilating something and this was the children expressing their ideas about something huge, about death or birth.

Judith – teacher

Back in the classroom we began exploring poetry. We discussed different styles and how the emotions within each poem were conveyed to the reader. Following a week of looking at poetry the children were shown visual images that could represent an aspect of birth, marriage or death and asked to write a phrase or word that captured their feelings about each picture. Children who had English as an additional language were encouraged to write in their own language. Following this the children were paired up and given one of the pictures with everyone's comments on it and asked to make a poem using the words and phrases. This was extremely successful and the poems produced were of higher standard than those produced before individually because the children had the whole classes' ideas as a resource. These poems and pictures formed the basis of the class book.

What was amazing was how every child came up with an original piece of work, even those who would usually just follow others and copy ideas. If somebody thought theirs was similar to somebody else's they went out of their way to make sure that theirs became different enough. The amount of thought they put into their work made the process really valuable because, although they were focused on the end product, in order to do what they wanted to do they had to put a lot into the process to make sure it said what they wanted to say. It was fascinating to watch.

There were children in that class who were underachieving in terms of literacy and could seldom express themselves. They had little confidence and for them to express themselves visually was a very powerful experience. Some of them chose not to talk about their work because it was too personal but those who did were far more articulate than they were in other situations. I think the sense of achievement this work gave them was far greater than any other piece of work. Ideas explored in art went into the writing. I think that's why it was so good. We used abstract images to stimulate the poetry and it was much more about expressing feelings and moods than about describing something. It was about their ideas and what death meant to them.

Year 4 textile from 2004

Judith – teacher

Next came trying to get children to think about symbols, how they are used and what messages they conveyed. We looked at various symbols and signs, ranging from traffic signs to logos. Then we asked the children to think of how people view birth, marriage and death and make a list. This was the challenging part as the children couldn't initially think about these in a deeper context. We had to push deeper by asking questions. eg.

Teacher: What are you thinking about?

Year 4 boy: Birth.

Teacher: So what happens when you are born?

Year 4 boy: You have life?

Teacher: So what is life?

Year 4 boy: You live.

Teacher: What do you mean by live?

Year 4 boy: You breathe and you do things.

Teacher: Is that life?

Year 4 boy: Miss how do I know what life is? I'm only 8.

Teacher: Well what do you think it will be like?

Year 4 boy: This is really hard.

Some time later, I discovered that the mother of one of the boys in the class had died. He and his family had decided to keep it from the school. When I found out I felt awful about what he had been going through and the fact that the school had done nothing. When I thought about the unit, I remembered the symbol he had made. He had chosen to represent the idea of going to heaven because that was an important aspect of death for him. I remembered how hard he had worked on his symbol; he spent ages trying to get it perfect. He had it in a state that I considered perfect for a long time and he just kept tweaking it and tweaking it and he was very defensive about anybody coming in his space or touching it.

I learnt not to be nervous. I tried to chant it and do what I was supposed to do.
Year 4 girl

Judith – teacher

These conversations took place with many of the children. For many of them the red hearts and rings were where they began and ended.

Teacher: What are you thinking about?

Year 4 girl: Marriage, Miss.

Teacher: So what is marriage?

Year 4 girl: It's when a man and a woman get married.

Teacher: Why do they get married?

Year 4 girl: They love each other. And they want children.

Teacher: Do they need to get married to do this?

Year 4 girl: No, but they are supposed to.

Teacher: Why are they supposed to?

Year 4 girl: Because people say they are supposed to.

Teacher: So what does getting married tell people then?

Year 4 girl: That people love each other.

Teacher: So do the man and woman stay together then?

Year 4 girl: Some do, some don't. It depends if they love each other.

Others, though, were able to think of cycles, doors opening and closing, and togetherness. The children were asked to design a symbol from their lists that they could make to convey their ideas.

Looking back, I realised that making that symbol was part of the whole process of him coming to terms with the death of his mother. That made me feel better because although I could have sat down and talked to him, the unit had given him the opportunity to think about and express something about what his mother's death meant to him without having to say anything or explain to anyone. We had given him a very powerful and moving tool. I realised afterwards that many of the children who focused on death were actually thinking about a specific bereavement.

In Religious Education we don't often give children the opportunity to deal with big concepts like parents remarrying or people dying. The work was non-threatening; they did not have to talk about anything they didn't want to, they did not have to explain in huge detail what the symbol meant. I think that was why some of them put so much into it: it was really about them and their personal lives and what they wanted to think about and explore.

Judith – teacher

Many of the designs were elaborate and some of the children had no idea how they would attempt to make their symbol. The skills we wanted the children to develop were about joining materials together. This involved cutting, gluing, taping and sewing. About 90% of the class had never threaded a needle, let alone sewn a stitch and this was a setback for our timescale, as we had to incorporate extra lessons to give the children some practice. Although we usually had at least two adults in the class, most of the time was spent threading 30 needles, and only a handful of children mastered this skill at the end. The children had to be watched while they glued and pieces of work had to be prised off the tables after copious amounts of glue, had been used. However, with a delay of about two weeks the children finally finished their individual symbols. We spent half a day discussing how we would compose our work on to a hanging. The children made choices about the final look of the piece, and its border, by laying their work out on the floor and viewing different options, before they agreed on a final arrangement.

It was fantastic to see how extremely proud the children were of their achievements. The final pieces looked fabulous and when the children read their poems in the book they were impressed with their achievements. Some who were more literate in English had acted as scribes for others, enabling everyone to express their ideas and make a valid contribution. The bilingual children were fascinated that their first language words had actually been used in the book and were proud to be asked what the words meant when others had forgotten.

The other – delightful – outcome was that all the symbols were put together as a class piece of art. I think it was the first time I had ever tried to produce a whole class piece. The process of negotiation and discussion about how they were going to arrange it was surprising. I thought they would be focused on their own part of it but, interestingly, they moved from thinking about their own symbols to thinking about the overall impact of their combined work. This developed a real sense of pride, community and unity in the class. The banner represented their different cultures, colours and ethnicities.

Many pupils had difficulty in creating their own symbols to represent the ideas behind ceremonies. Some got very frustrated and a few were reduced to tears. All staff involved supported the pupils' thinking and discussed ways in through thinking about colour, feel or shape.

Some pupils found it difficult to know what they might do and did not have the vocabulary for describing what they wanted to do.

Teachers' evaluation, week 1 and 2

> I found it difficult when I was planning my symbol because at first I didn't know what to do and then I had an idea in my head once I drew some circles on my paper and then I drew an angry tear here in the middle. *Year 4 pupil*

The fact that it was displayed first in the class then in the school gave them a sense of pride especially with all the excitement afterwards. The poetry was performed at the launch of the new RE syllabus and was highlighted as excellent practice. Illustrations of the work were placed in the Standing Advisory Council for Religious Education Syllabus and the hangings went to the Borough Art Exhibition. That was such a transformation from the soul destroying process of repeatedly teaching the same content, to being held up as a role model in the borough. The advisor said it was a very good example of pupils having the opportunity to think about their own spirituality.

The children really felt they were artists and that they had produced a piece of work that others valued. I think you only need that to happen once for you to understand the value of your own artwork, that other people take it seriously. It doesn't have to happen every year. For those children, at that point, it changed the way they viewed art. They became more confident and they became closer as a class. It had a knock-on effect over the rest of the year, particularly in terms of thinking processes, because of the challenge of developing an understanding of abstract concepts. This enabled them to think more abstractly in other contexts too.

I never felt that impact in any other unit. Once the children had done it the first time, I think that the impact lessened. There would never be the same transition because they would know that you could link things and explore

> Some found it hard to plan their work without handling the materials. They found exploratory work difficult and tended to have one idea and use it rather than build on it.
>
> Pupils were able to use more appropriate vocabulary for explaining their work and some could explain their reasoning. Some made choices based on personal preference whereas others struggled to explain
>
> Pupils are becoming more confident about talking about their learning. Some can now describe what they learnt and how but others are still struggling to articulate it.
>
> *Teachers' evaluation, week 3 and 4*

ideas in that way. That first time was such a breakthrough it made me feel much more enthusiastic and capable as a teacher. There were times when I thought we would never get finished and then all the effort would be wasted and the children would feel failures. It was a changing point in my career.

For Fred and Chantelle, who had special educational needs, it was a real boost because they were visual learners and could express themselves through pattern. Both had a really strong sense of what they wanted to express. They didn't like drawing, they didn't think they were good at it, but when you gave them objects that they could manipulate they felt very comfortable doing that. I think it's probably something they had been doing since nursery and that they considered 'playing' and this was the first time it was validated. They created something that meant something and they realised you don't always have to write something down.

> **Death**
>
> It's like a symbol that is blurry and in another world
>
> With a language beginning by a person dying
>
> It is a puzzle to a new world that nobody understands
>
> It is like a drawing getting messed up with no meaning
>
> Looking like a journey with a new map
>
> It is a trail to a mysterious world
>
> That nobody understands
>
> *Year 4 pupil*

The fact that you can't write independently doesn't mean you don't have anything to say. Chantelle came into that class saying, 'I can't read, I can't write, I'm stupid and I don't know anything'. At the end of that project, although she often changed the meaning of the symbol, she could give a good explanation of what it meant every time and talk clearly about why she had used what she used and why she had arranged them in that way. It was a really striking symbol that stood out even in the whole class piece. She still had a long way to go in terms of self-esteem but the project started to push her in the right direction in terms of her valuing the contribution she could make in the class.

The children were questioned about what they had learned through the process and their answers were recorded as follows:

Knowledge

- stitching is not easy – you think it's going to be easy but when you start it's not.
- new vocabulary
- how to join fabrics
- how to sew
- how to stitch different patterns
- how to do a knot
- how to plan work

Attitude

- perseverance
- friends helped each other
- being careful
- concentration
- believing in yourself

Skills

- how to use different materials together to make symbols
- how to create a former
- how to bend wire in a zigzag
- how to thread a needle
- to sew without pricking yourself
- how to decorate an art object
- stencils – how to use one
- how to stitch evenly
- how to stitch different materials

What did not help or was difficult

- stitching flat materials
- I rushed my work
- I could not get a neat edge
- getting it to look how I wanted
- I was not satisfied with my work
- sometimes what you do is not how you thought it would look
- it was difficult some things were dangerous (needles)
- being worried about what would happen next
- some people were pushing
- some people were talking about things other than work
- it was difficult to concentrate

Understanding

- how to stick things together by cutting and folding
- how to cut card and cover with fabric
- how to sew around in a circle
- different materials suit different purposes
- how to make something how you want it
- being careful and trying hard
- the value of sketching and planning
- how to represent ideas (heart with two things touching)

We learnt by

- thinking
- looking
- remembering teaching
- watching someone
- trying

The Impact on pupils with special educational needs
– Amanda Wilson

The creativity programme gave some pupils with special educational needs an opportunity to come into their own, becoming the expert in the class. For others it created an environment where they could freely explore the use of a range of creative skills without feeling threatened by the fact that their academic skills were less developed than their peers'.

Year 5 Projects

During my time as a Year 5 teacher, I have taught pupils with a range of learning needs, ranging from pupils with severe behaviour issues, which meant that they were only in the mainstream school setting for two days a week, to specific learning difficulties such as autism or dyslexia. It was interesting to observe how some of these pupils responded to the different projects. The combination of academic and creative lessons meant it was possible to make differentiation more explicit and in some cases, create tailor-made activities to suit the needs of the pupil.

Over the years four creative learning units were developed for Year 5. These linked Geography with Design and Technology, History with Drama, Science with Design and Technology, Dance with Personal, Social, Health and Citizenship Education.

The Geography unit culminated in a tangible end product, benefitting pupils who needed to have concrete evidence of their learning. This, I think, provided the best opportunities for pupils in my class with special needs. The aim was to take a close look at the local area, land use and changes over time. Following a series of visits to local landmarks where observations were carried out, the pupils looked at maps of the area focusing on the position of landmarks and identifying their key features. This culminated in the pupils

---

Afua, parent

I find with him that he is very boisterous but he finds it very calming when he is doing the arts. He changes completely and it's boosted his confidence. Even though he is boisterous he is not a very confident child. Getting involved in the arts has boosted his confidence a lot and I find he has calmed down.

There are more positives than negatives. I am just saying that in everything there are advantages and disadvantages and with this the advantages would outweigh the disadvantages

> **Lorraine, Teaching Assistant**
>
> I think that creative learning has taught children how to appreciate each other's work.

working in small groups to create a three-dimensional textile representation of the local area.

Neelam was a pupil who had been diagnosed as having dyslexia and during regular curriculum lessons she often had difficulty accessing the activities without specific differentiation and support. She rarely contributed to class discussion and was often the one receiving help from peers. During our Geography and Design and Technology unit she came into her own. It turned out that she had a real talent for sewing and needlework. Suddenly the tables were turned and she became the helper, rather than the one receiving help. She became more vocal and relished having the opportunity to help other

> **Lucy, Ethnic Minority Achievement Co-ordinator**
>
> Even though children who are learning English don't necessarily have special educational needs we have found that creative learning approaches support their access to the curriculum. There is a significant cross-over between creative learning and good teaching for developing English.
>
> There was a Turkish boy in year 5 who had been in the school about a year and was at the beginning stages of learning English. When they first began the music around the world unit where they make musical instruments he wasn't particularly keen on doing it. The teacher asked them to bring music from home and some of them bought musical instruments and some bought tapes. She deliberately played some Turkish music and his face lit up. She asked him to go home and speak to his parents and he brought back a tape and decided he would make a drum. He had seen a picture and he had talked to his parents and he was really enthusiastic. So by bringing in his culture the staff made him want to be involved in the learning and he finished it and performed for everybody.
>
> When I was working in year 2 while Stephen was working with them on dance and emotions, we had two newly arrived pupils from Lithuania. They had no English at all. I spoke to Stephen beforehand about these pupils and I could just see their little faces watching the others because it was so visual and so practical. We read *The Tunnel*, then did some drama and made facial expressions, then made some word banks in English and Lithuanian. They accessed it so well. They didn't need the words to take part in the dances – they could just use their faces and their bodies and it was wonderful. It didn't matter what stage of learning English they were at, they could access that lesson equally with the rest of the class.

children realise their ideas. The creative learning approach encourages children to evaluate and work on their ideas collaboratively in order to develop them and this pupil found she could support others through this process.

The way we worked on these units enabled me to learn more about the children in the class. They were more self-directed in this unit and the work was very practical so we saw them from a different point of view. We were becoming more analytical about the learning process and focusing more on learning than teaching. We were looking more closely at the children. For example Dale was a pupil in my class who seemed to have an overwhelming need to align objects just so. This became more apparent during our Geography and Design and Technology unit. Whilst tidying up at the end of one session, he seemed to take unnecessarily long to complete his task of collecting cotton reels and putting them in their boxes. On closer inspection it became evident that he was ordering the cotton reels; arranging them in specific categories in the box, totally focused on his task.

On another occasion Dale had been asked by members of his group to undertake a specific task, which would not have presented a challenge to most of the pupils. He found it quite difficult, but rather than communicate this to his group, he became distracted, walking around the classroom with no real purpose. When I identified the problem I was able to negotiate an approach that he found more accessible. This enabled him to become more involved in the project and play an important role in his group. These events triggered further observations and eventually led to an assessment by an autistic specialist, who identified him as having specific language and communication difficulties. He was later referred to the Speech and Language team.

Throughout the school there have been similar examples of the ways in which pupils with special needs have responded to different units of work and it has given us greater insight into those children's learning. It has also enabled us to respond differently to their learning needs and provide more appropriate and accessible opportunities.

One of the Teaching Assistants supported a Year 1 autistic pupil. Abi enjoyed tactile and practical tasks, could be very demanding in class but did not communicate verbally other than through noises. The unit the class was working on gave the pupils opportunities to think about different aspects of themselves. It allowed Abi to develop her sense of self and her place in the classroom. For the first time she actually worked physically in a group. Although she did not communicate verbally with the other children she was in the same space as they were. Before that point she had tended to be isolated because of the difficulties she experienced in relating to other pupils. At the end of the unit the pupils created a self-portrait. She became deeply engrossed in the work, managing to sit and focus for much longer periods than usual. The impact this particular unit had on Abi made staff working alongside her more

Christine, teaching assistant

With the activity we did last year on the senses, I was working with a child who was autistic. She got quite involved in it all. She could relate to it because she had a nose and ears and eyes. She was more focused on the activity; there was more concentration because she enjoyed what she was doing, she was creating herself. For that child to actually sit at an activity, that was amazing to me.

She was able to point to the finished piece of work and say her name. She had recognised her own piece of work. There is usually very little verbal communication; I had never actually heard her voice before. For her to actually say her name – everyone picked up on it. In the long run I couldn't say if there was long term impact but every time she recognised her picture she obviously remembered that she did this. I'd say what's this and she'd point to her nose and things like that and she would say nose. I had never heard her name any part of her body, hands, feet, nothing. Just to communicate with her in words, although it was just single words, you were getting a response from her, which was a real achievement for her.

When I supported another boy the year before, I think it was when we were doing marbling, he thoroughly enjoyed that hands on experience and he enjoyed dripping the paint, I think it was oils, into the water and making patterns. His fine motor skills, they're not very good and for him to get involved in something like that and enjoy it, we could build on that to involve him in other activities.

I've also worked with children who have English as an additional language and the activity we did this year with the clear sheets – acetates – and they had to draw pictures from the music, from imagination. Some of them couldn't form letters but the pictures they put together from listening to music were amazing, I really enjoyed working with them for that. They loved it, they were asking if they could do it again and asking is it my turn: so much imagination. I would say that a few of the children who had very little English, the way they tried to explain what their picture was about and they tried hard to communicate, their language definitely improved.

When you asked them what the picture was about they were telling you their own story, where they had come from and their own family. It was one of the best projects I've worked on with the children; it was more rewarding for me as well. They were all rewarding in a way because you can see the children enjoyed it. Other groups like the higher ability groups, some of their work was fantastic. The imagination that went into it, listening to the music and giving them time to think, real thought went into drawing the pictures. They even thought about the colours, a lot of work went into that.

Helani, teacher

All children get an opportunity to take part and enjoy more active and creative lessons. They don't have to be able to speak English well or be good at literacy to show they are learning well in any particular unit. They have become more used to working with each other in various situations. Everyone works together and communicates with each other. Working in more mixed ability groups offers the children the opportunity to share their learning with others even if they are not confident when talking and or writing.

aware of the type of activities best suited to her; it provided them with an opportunity to plan more effectively for her future learning.

Linda, a Teaching Assistant working in Year 3, highlighted the way in which the creative learning approach is able to cater for different learning needs. She commented on how a Science and Dance unit in year 3 made learning more accessible and how pupils were able to gain a far better understanding of this topic from the dances they were creating. They used scientific language and concepts related to magnets and springs as a starting point for creating a dance. It was far more effective in developing their understanding than experimenting within the confines of the classroom.

Two other pupils in particular were identified as displaying totally different characteristics than normal during creative units. George was diagnosed with Attention Deficit and Hyperactivity Disorder and was often boisterous in and

Faye, teacher

if I think about last year, when they made those musical instruments specifically with George because he had behaviour problems, I honestly thought there were going to be nails in children's heads and children with broken fingers and all sorts. But in fact it had the opposite affect on him: he was incredibly calm working with all the tools and not only was he really calm but he would go up to other children without being prompted and offer them advice and say maybe you could try this or do that. So it was really nice to see him interacting with other kids and them accepting his help rather than saying 'Oh god he's going to beat me up'. So, in terms of specific children I think, bizarrely, the children it probably helped the most were in fact the children I thought it would help least.

Andi is another example. He is rather disruptive in class, but when it was anything to do with music or poetry he was quite different. If you think generally about the musical instruments unit he behaved better because he enjoyed those subjects. So I think it has had an impact on the kids in terms of enriching their lives, and the same with the staff.

Andi, Director SW Newham EAZ

When Manor and Star School Councils are in action outside school, their articulation of learning and the way they pose questions and interpret answers is more advanced than some of their peers. That's a reflection of the development of one of the key skills – questioning. There is depth to the questions that Manor and Star School Councils ask, at EAZ Citizenship meetings for instance. As chair of the School Councils Question Time I have to answer those questions and they really challenge me and the panel.

Other anecdotal evidence has come from visitors to both schools who, when they have engaged in conversation with the children about their learning, have been surprised at their ability to articulate and describe it.

out of class. He attended a behavioural unit three days a week. The creative unit the pupils were involved in linked Science with Music and its aim was to develop pupils' understanding of sound and how it related to musical instruments. The pupils had to design and make their own musical instrument. Before this project started the class teacher had visions of him running around the classroom, disrupting others. She was pleasantly surprised by his calm and focused demeanour. This unexpected result was attributed to the fact that he had complete ownership over what he was doing; he was creating what he wanted for himself.

Some pupils with special needs are working at a level below that of their peers and consequently lack confidence in their ability to learn. The creative learning units provide pupils with opportunities to access the curriculum in different ways and produce positive results. This develops their confidence.

How do you think the creative curriculum has supported pupil learning?

- I think it gives the pupils a good foundation for later learning
- I am not sure how it will prepare them for secondary school because they tend to work in very different ways and I think that sometimes our pupils might be seen as challenging because they are used to questioning.
- I think it makes the curriculum more interesting and engages the pupils more, Looking at the curriculum through Multiple Intelligences helps the children learn more. They learn more about other things.
- I think the links between different curriculum areas are stronger and tighter than they were in the 70s.
- I think that creative curriculum skills can be used in other areas and be taken on into later life.

Feedback from a governor's discussion

What do the pupils say? – *Catherine McGill*

For four years we have asked Key Stage 2 and Year 2 pupils to fill in an annual questionnaire about their thinking about the curriculum and this has provided us with a database. This helps us to evaluate the work we are doing from their perspective. We have also talked more often with small groups of children in an effort to assess the impact of the work and to offer them opportunities to suggest improvements. We have asked parents to complete questionnaires to try and find out if they noticed any impact from the individual units, changes in their children's behaviour, learning or ability to communicate.

The pupils' questionnaire gives them a chance to say what they are enjoying and to comment on their learning in both the curriculum subjects and the arts. The pupils' responses have steadily improved over the last four years. That can probably be attributed to the greater emphasis we are placing on reflective learning.

The questions of most relevance are: What do you enjoy? What helps you learn? What can you learn from the arts?

What do children most enjoy?

The most common responses to this question were

- learning is visible to them
- relevance – they can see the point of what they are doing
- they like active and physical engagement
- they can make their own choices or use their own ideas
- exploration: mistakes are seen as learning opportunities
- content varies within the subject areas
- they can pursue personal preferences for particular subjects

Providing opportunities for children to use and develop their own ideas can be a challenge in the classroom, with all the pressures of testing, the curriculum and organisation and planning, but both pupils and teachers recog-

---

Violet and Lucy, teachers

The units have allowed children to explore and learn from their mistakes and this gives them confidence. Concentrating on the process rather than the product also helps. Children are developing skills they can transfer to other subjects.

> I liked making the musical instruments because we had a lot of freedom. When the teacher talks you just get bored and you are not doing anything. *Year 5 child*

Jackie, parent

I've got a little boy in year 1. Working in art definitely makes a difference. It gives them more confidence, helps them explore different media and gives them a wider outlook on things. It encourages them a lot ... When you look at them in nursery they are far more confident than we were at 3 or 4. Then you go up and look at the 4/5 year olds and they are more confident and more worldly. It is having an impact on their self-esteem.

---

nise the value of such opportunities. It gives pupils a sense of control and ownership over their learning.

What helps learning?

The responses suggest the children think that the way we are trying to work helps them learn well. The things they find helpful are opportunities to work collaboratively and learn from each other; being able to make choices; asking questions; trying their best.

When thinking about their learning, pupils sometimes mentioned the product and made evaluative comments about it or about the process they went through.

> The teacher shows you all different things that you can do and then you practise them and choose which moves you want to do. *Year 5 child*
>
> I think I learnt well in Design and Technology because you get to think of your own ideas. *Year 5 child*
>
> If there is something you don't like about what you have done you can go back and see if you could change anything to make it better. *Year 5 child*
>
> You have to listen, active listening and then when it is your turn you can copy her. (referring to responses to modelling). *Year 6 child*
>
> Design and Technology was great because we made our musical instruments and the thing that made me learn better was if we went wrong the teacher didn't tell us exactly what to do, so if we made a mistake we like cleared our mess up by ourselves. *Year 5 child*

Children are listening to each other's ideas.

Children are becoming more independent and their confidence is growing.

Academically less able children feel their ideas are being valued, they seem full of ideas and contributions.

Children are able to recognise what they are learning and how they are learning.

Notes from teacher discussion

Some pupils referred to teacher modelling as being a helpful strategy and referred to watching and listening followed by doing. Success in these situations depended on the quality of the watching and listening. A number of pupils also said they found clear explanations helpful.

Some children also recognised that evaluating their work helped them to learn well.

What can you learn from the arts?

The vast majority of the pupils were able to identify some learning in the arts and only a few could not or did not. Most of the learning they described related to specific skills or knowledge in each particular art form.

In music the pupils were able to describe specific skills learnt and were especially articulate about learning instruments. Some of those engaged in Samba and African drumming lessons made links between music and movement. There were also pupils who identified the links between movement and music when talking about dance,.

One pupil identified the role of evaluation in dance, saying that being able to change and develop ideas in the light of reflection was useful when learning dance; another saw dance as an expressive form.

Elizabeth, parent

In school I find that art is very important for kids. It makes them more active and the things they do in art they enjoy, and they come home and tell you about what they have done and I will ask them questions about what they have learnt and they always have something to answer, so I think arts are important in every kid's life.

Josie, parent

I think they express themselves; they can communicate with you more.

Petra, teacher

I said, 'here is some information – go and record it how you think.' They found it really hard but they enjoyed the freedom of being able to choose. I think if they can record it in a way that makes sense to them, it helps them to order their thinking.'

Violet, teacher

Trial and error helps them learn, where they make mistakes and then they think about their mistakes, it gives them ownership. It also places the emphasis on the process rather than the product.

One aspect of learning that was identified in drama was that you could find out that there were many ways of doing the same thing. Similarly pupils thought that in art you could learn that there are many different ways of working.

Pupils identify their gains from involvement with the arts as:

- raised levels of confidence.
- development of collaborative and team work skills
- development of imagination and creativity
- specific arts skills they might use in the future
- opportunities to try out ideas

In an ideal world, we want all pupils to enjoy what they are doing and feel that they are learning successfully. Our responsibility is to provide a broad and balanced curriculum that offers pupils a range of experiences that will support the development of the skills and understanding they need to deal with a rapidly changing society. The pupils identified the following in their responses: the ability to communicate and collaborate; perseverance; flexibility; creativity; imagination; an understanding that there is more than one way to do things; independent thinking. The responses from pupils indicate that they identify the value of the arts in promoting the development of these skills and aptitudes.

Sue, parent

I think it does make a difference in the fact that it's another thing that they are doing here aside from literacy and numeracy. Like you were saying it's a confidence thing as well. A lot of the children who would sit back and not answer a question will get up and show a dance or show a model they have been doing.

The thing that helps me learn well is interacting with other people and sharing their ideas. *Year 6 child*

It went well because everyone had a contribution about what they thought... it helped me to learn more because I got other people's ideas. *Year 4 child*

I think they (the arts) are similar because when you are doing drama it's your imagination that helps and in dance, art and music it's your imagination as well. *Year 5 child*

You get like a boost of confidence. *Year 4 child*

You learn to like turn your thoughts and feelings into a dance. *Year 5 child*

Sam, parent

Another thing was that she was working with other people who, although they were in her class and had been probably for four years, she hadn't really got to know or talk to, but [now] she had to. They were put in different groups and they met different people. That helped my daughter a lot. I wonder if it's because of the arts or because of the projects and they way they mixed people up.

Dlane, parent

With Lucy it has made her more confident because she is a quiet child. It has helped her in that sense. I came in when they had Discover here – it's a bit hard to get here because of work. I think it was very good, they were getting the kids involved and bringing them out of themselves and letting their inhibitions go and do things that they felt. I think it was good.

Donna, parent

I suppose that the children all work in different ways, they learn things in different ways. With Jack he's less academic. So him doing things that are more physical he can take things in and learn better. When they made puppets and they did that show at the theatre, he really enjoyed that and it was a good way for him to learn.

Sue, parent

They can work individually but then you can set them a group task and they all do muck in and it's as I said, there is no right or wrong, so they can all have their own input. They all work well together. There is nobody who can turn round and say that's not really right.

Laura, parent

It helps their co-ordination and they need that as well. That's probably why with dance he never used to move much but lately he's been moving differently, wiggling his bottom and doing things with his arms. He's been coming out with poems. He did a poem about me and that was quite nice and he does something with music, the violin, he likes that and now he wants to try something else. My brother has got a drum kit and he wants to learn that but my brother says ' wait till you've done it in school'. He started liking music a lot more. I thought it was because he was getting older but obviously it's because he has been doing it in school. He didn't have all this in his old school and he does like to try new things but sometimes he needs a push.

Conclusion

Everyone concerned with the pupils' learning, including the pupils, see significant outcomes from the approach we have been developing. Petra and Judith's descriptions resonate with the definition of creativity in *All Our Futures* (1999). There are still tensions between the kinds of learning being described and improved results in standard attainment tests. This is an issue that we continue to struggle with and are unlikely to resolve soon.

3
PARTNERSHIPS WITH ARTS ORGANISATIONS
'I enjoyed it because I got to meet new people and see what they could do'

This chapter explores the nature of some of the partnerships in which we have been involved. Michelle Wilson, Assistant Head and Arts co-ordinator provides an overview. And music co-ordinator Leesa Harbottle, describes our involvement in the Wider Opportunities Pilot Scheme

Partnerships – *Michelle Wilson*

Throughout the development of the creative learning and curriculum reform, we have been able to forge links with a variety of organisations, art galleries, arts providers, artists and museums. These links have been an integral part of

---

Conversation between parents and a family support worker

Laura: We were in the nursery when a man came in with a book to share. We had to get up and dance

Brenda: It was a special story and it's really helped the children they were very happy.

Laura: We had to think about where he had travelled and we had to do different dances from Africa and places like that.

Brenda: I really enjoyed it. It was great fun.

Sara: So even as adults you are enjoying physical learning. The children get a lot more out of physical learning.

Laura: It was nice to spend the time with them, to relax and have fun with them.

Sara: The good thing there is that it's good for the children to see the parents still learning. That's really good for their learning.

Conversation with Donna, nursery teacher and Razia, nursery nurse

Donna: What makes the difference is good planning, good interaction and team-work between the artist and the staff and an ability to communicate with children. I also think you need to be able to evaluate and identify problems and then solve them. I think with one artist communication broke down and we completely misunderstood each other and it wasn't rectified.

Razia: Yes, when we evaluated after each session and talked about what went well and what next, that made it work well.

the journey and the experience of creative learning for the children, staff and parents in both schools. With the school budgets being so restricted, forging relationships with external providers and having the opportunity to link with local artists is not always an expense schools can cover. But our schools have various ways of obtaining funding and making these partnerships possible. We bid for specific grants and work in some partnerships where the arts provider funds the school and gallery-based activities. There are also galleries and organisations that provide free opportunities for pupils.

The starting up, running and evaluation of these partnerships demands extra time, work and effort. For partnership to be successful, careful preparation is essential. Issues such as joint planning, agreed protocols, agreed budgets and project dates all need to be addressed. This requires huge commitment from the artists, partners and staff at the school. If the partnerships are successfully run, the impact and benefits are great and the hard work pays dividends.

Linking with partners and types of partnerships

Links between our schools and external providers are set up in various ways. We have been approached by organisations that obtained our details through the Local Authority, through word of mouth or flyers; we have responded to e-mails, government initiatives such as Education Action Zones, Excellence in Cities and the Neighbourhood Renewal Fund. We also identify areas of priority from the school development plan and find partners to support them, where appropriate.

Projects range in length, spanning half terms or, in some cases, the whole academic year. We have also engaged in long-term partnerships that have extended over three years, such as our partnerships with Newham Academy of Music and Creative Partnerships London East. Dance and poetry residencies ran for a year or more. Shorter collaborations have tended to be year group related and for a specific purpose.

Petra, class teacher

They finally got a sense of poetry as a form of self-expression. It's hard to explain the difference between narrative and poetry. By linking poetry with another subject area the children have the opportunity to express an idea through poetry and they start to realise why a poet is a poet. In the same way they get a sense of why painters paint and why sculptors sculpt. It's hard to work on poetry within the confines of the literacy hour because you read a poet's work and you take elements of it and replicate it and that's not how poets work. I felt a real sense of real poetry when we did the bullying project but it was only when we worked with a local poet, Charlie Dark, and I heard him talking to the children about why he was a poet and how he wrote poetry, that I realised what we had done was real poetry. We had started with an emotive idea and expressed it through poetry. If you take a poem about a train in literacy and then use the same rhymes and structure to write about something else, that is not poetry. It's a literacy activity and it is valid but it is not poetry as a form of self-expression; it's not what poets do.

I understand a wider spectrum of art now because I understand a bit more about where the artist is coming from, not necessarily exactly but that they will have gone through a process to express something that matters to them. I enjoy poetry more now because I understand that poets have something to say and they have selected their words very carefully. I think that's why when we have done poetry in the creative units, I feel very proud of it. The children have genuinely gone through that same process of thinking about what they want to say and having to select the vocabulary and structure to express it in the best way. They haven't necessarily been looking for rhymes. It's been more real because we haven't said 'ok now do this in 20 minutes'. We've taken different starting points and approached it in different ways and in the end the children have picked the poems that mean the most to them and the ones that express their ideas the best. They begin to see themselves as poets. If you can get children to write a poem as a poet rather than as a literacy exercise I think it is guaranteed to produce better poetry. They will feel more confident and happier with the results.

We have been fortunate to establish links with organisations such as the Craft Council, which provided us with a series of one or two day sessions, in which children attended an exhibition and then created a piece of work with a member of the art gallery staff. Such partnerships are not necessarily linked to curriculum learning objectives or school development plans, but still form an integral part of the children's learning experiences. The links with galleries and museums often come about through staff members attending teacher evenings that are regularly advertised in flyers and bulletins sent to schools.

Staff in both schools have benefitted from working with external providers and artists. Some artists brought in specialist skills and understanding of their

School Council

Specialists come for lots of things, for example dance, drama, poetry and art. They help us by teaching us something fun and linking it with a curriculum subject, for example dance and science.

The specialists also teach us things that they are better at than our teachers. This helps us learn more and we gain even more interest in the subject.

art form that teachers don't have. Combining the artist's skills and knowledge of the art form with the teacher's knowledge and understanding of the learning process in planning for projects has enriched the professional development of our teaching and support staff.

Planning, preparation and communication

For a partnership to be successful, planning, preparation and communication are vital before, during and after the project. Both the artist and the schools have to be clear on the aims and objectives of the project. What is it that we want to achieve by undertaking this work? What do we want the children to experience and learn through this partnership?

Once a link has been set up with an artist or organisation, the intended aims and outcomes, as well as logistical issues, are discussed at the first meeting: an idea of the time scale, the number of meetings and sessions entailed, costs, who will supply the materials needed and dates for planning and evaluation meetings during and after the project. With most of the partnerships we have a written partnership agreement. This is to ensure that the expectations of all involved are clearly understood. Especially when a great deal of money is being invested, both parties need to be entirely clear about their role in the project, what they are expected to provide and the expected outcomes.

Copyright and ownership are increasingly important. Who owns the rights to the photographs or work created during the project? Permission to take and use photographs of pupils involved in the project also needs to be granted by parents and guardians.

Linda, teacher

One creative learning unit focused on making puppets. Together with the artists, we planned carefully and agreed to use a much loved book, *Here Come the Aliens!* We got some fantastic work from the children; we had a planet base, two big lunar modules, rockets, stars and alien puppets. It was a hands-on project with a colourful outcome. The children absolutely loved it. It affected them all but particularly those with English as an additional language, who could talk about and describe what they had done. The tool of creative learning enabled them to access the book more easily and to express themselves. It gave them a way into literacy. They could choose what they did; there was a freedom in the way it was set up. The relaxed atmosphere meant they did not feel pressured, they didn't feel that they had to join in the making and achieve an outcome. There was no right or wrong way to do things. The project developed their imagination.

One of the children for whom English was an additional language also had behaviour problems when he first came to the school. Through this creative learning unit he channelled his energies into the project and it had a lasting impact on him. He became really engaged in the work and it helped him to build more positive relationships with his peers.

The artists were very enthusiastic and that of course fired our own enthusiasm. It was infectious. I think one of the key principles was our having planned it in advance with the artist. At the end of each session or day we regrouped, thought about what happened, what went well and what we might do tomorrow. Interestingly, when we had the Artsmark assessor round to look at the work and talk to the children about what they had done, two of the children who gave her the most information were two emerging bilingual pupils. They wanted to converse with her and found that they could. They went over to her and patted her and said 'I want to talk to you,' and she had no choice really but to take the time to listen because they were so enthusiastic and she was caught up by their enthusiasm. The children need to own the project otherwise creativity is not going to happen. That is why the puppet unit was most successful: the children ended up leading it.

How the work is linked to the curriculum

Because we needed to develop particular curriculum areas significantly we set up longer-term partnerships too. Curriculum needs were identified through consultation and evaluation of teaching and learning and agreed by senior leadership teams. One example is the partnership we set up with dance artist Stephen Mason. The staff in both schools staff were not confident about teaching dance, so a year-long dance residency was set up, paid for partly by funding by Creative Partnerships London East and partly from school funds.

Each year group identified a curriculum area to be linked with dance. For example Year 6 linked it to environmental issues in Geography, Year 3 linked it with the Science topic of forces and magnets and the Nursery linked it to a storybook. Each unit was planned by the class teachers and the dance artists together. Before the artists' visits, class teachers delivered subject content. The subject knowledge was then built on through the dance lessons. After each weekly dance session, pupils completed follow up work in individual, class or group learning journals. Teachers would then introduce the next objectives to the class in preparation for the following dance lesson.

Each year group worked with the dance artist for one half term. Each project was evaluated throughout and on completion. At these evaluation meetings, the original aims and objectives were referred to, as well as the intended knowledge and skills gained by the pupils. Planning was modified if the pupils needed more consolidation of particular topics or concepts.

Shorter-term projects were also curriculum linked, for example, a Year 2 literacy unit based on story telling and story writing. For this two-week

---

Sue, teaching assistant and parent

I think it was when John was in Year 2 and I was working here at the time and they did the puppets project. They made the puppets and they wrote a story and they went to the Angel Theatre to watch a puppet show.

From my point of view, as a teaching assistant, we went through the same process as the children; we went to a workshop at Manor School and made the puppets and I was involved in that side of it.

It was brilliant, the whole thing, because with the children who had difficulties with reading and writing they could still tell their story using the puppets. They could talk about how they made the puppets, how they moved the puppets. It was a really, really good project. I loved that one. The children were really involved.

> *Lisle, deputy head*
>
> There were some issues with the organisation and planning of the puppet project in Year 2. Despite this I think some very good outcomes came about because the children still talk about it. If Year 5 are still talking about something they did in Year 2 that means they had a really good experience and it impacted on their learning.

> I was making the spider bigger, it made everyone scream, it got bigger and bigger and I was spinning the spider around
>
> Year 2 pupil

project, we formed a partnership with the Little Angel Puppet Theatre. The children visited the theatre to watch a production. Puppeteers ran a series of workshops in which they made puppets with the children. Together with the class teachers, the children wrote stories and used their puppets to perform their own show at the Theatre.

Impact of partnerships

Collaborating with external artists is essential in guaranteeing a broader learning experience for the children. It broadens their outlook, giving them opportunities to see artists at work, and enables them to begin to see themselves as an artist. Partly as a result, they attach higher status to what they do. Working with artists also affects staff professional development. It helps staff improve their own skills in the arts, to understand more about learning in the arts and to develop teaching strategies and helps the artists gain greater understanding of the learning process.

> *Petra, teacher*
>
> That year my group were involved in a project with a gallery. The children's knowledge, skills and expectations were more advanced than the artists had expected. The work they were doing wasn't very engaging, they were able to go through far more complex processes.
>
> What amazed me about that was that when their work was displayed in the gallery at the end, it didn't overwhelm the children. They thought it was fair enough, they thought 'This a place for art, we made art so our work is here.'

Table 3. The A+ Protocol for Teacher-Artist Collaboration

Brokering
- greater autonomy for schools, within brokered partnerships to select artists according to the schools requirements
- artists selected need to have the ability to understand age-appropriate teaching methods and to provide clear lesson structures
- specialised teams of artists to be created, where possible, to maximise impact and sustainability of projects
- a Learning Contract to be made between teachers and artists incorporating clear learning objectives for both groups

Pre – Project Planning
- dedicated planning time for artists to include opportunities for classroom observation
- development of Inset models that provide opportunities for teachers to acquire art skills and to help them participate in sessions
- clear liaison on project objectives and starting points
- dialogue between artists and teachers over roles, responsibilities and understandings of effective practice regarding the arts and learning
- the organisational structure of the school to be acknowledged in operational planning by the arts organisation

Project Planning
- ongoing evaluation as part of project delivery. Meetings to include artists and all staff, including teaching assistants, involved with the project
- team-teaching for artists to allow greater flexibility

Project Delivery
- greater planned integration of teachers in session delivery, to increase confidence in arts skills and build professional mobility, trust and mutual professional respect between teachers and artist
- evidence of lesson plans and structure to be provided by the artist and shared with teachers
- evidence of project work to be clearly displayed by teachers throughout the project

Performance
- the pressure to prepare for performance at the cost of learning must be avoided – focus on process not product
- any performance must have clear learning objectives

Post-performance
- artists to take part in evaluative discussions with staff, children and senior leadership teams

Klara, student on the graduate teacher programme

It was very inspiring to work with a drama specialist as part of this year's creative learning project. The drama activities really helped the children with their writing skills and developed their imaginations especially in relation to fantasy worlds. They were able to evaluate their work by looking at the videos and photographs taken in the sessions, that gave them instant feedback. They used them in both literacy and history.

Tensions

We have encountered certain issues, such as

- artists not understanding the pupils' needs, in terms of keeping the pace tight and moving the children's learning on
- arriving at the right time in the right place and allowing enough preparation time
- ensuring that planning is undertaken and shared with the adults in the school
- ensuring that police checks are done in advance of school visits

After the first few partnerships we drew up our own protocol to help us avoid some of the pitfalls.

Our Musical Journey – *Leesa Harbottle, music coordinator*

The start of our musical journey

In the year our schools began their commitment to creative learning, we also started another exciting journey. We became pilot schools for the Wider Opportunities Music Initiative, which explored different methods and structures that would support the provision of instrumental learning to every primary pupil in the country. A music project, albeit more modest, was already established in Star school. Children throughout the school were introduced to rhythm and pitch, and developed listening, vocal skills and notation in three twenty-minute lessons taught every week in addition to regular music lessons. Because of our involvement in the creative learning partnership, we were invited to be the two schools in Newham, out of 49 nationally, to take part in the pilot.

Teri, headteacher

I was very excited to be involved in this because although we had a lot of music in the school we did not have the opportunity for all children to learn an instrument. I thought the idea of having musicians who were also teachers working alongside our teachers would actually enable us as a school to develop our understanding of music. I did not know much about the Kodaly system but I discussed it with the music co-ordinator and we had looked at what they were doing at Star. We had already decided we wanted to develop that approach at Manor.

I was also excited by the fact that it was a pilot and fitted in with the way we were working with different artists. The fact that it was going to be monitored by Her Majesty's Inspectors (HMI) meant that we would be able to tap into expertise we would not normally have access to.

The first year

Initially, the whole school continued with our already established music project and our Year 3 classes were involved in the Wider Opportunities programme. They received General Musicianship lessons once a week from a visiting teacher from Newham Academy of Music and the class teachers followed these lessons up every day. After two terms, the children were given the opportunity to learn to play an instrument. In one school two classes had recorders and one had violins. In the other school one class had recorders and one had keyboards. The format remained the same, with daily whole class lessons led by the regular class teacher and weekly input from visiting musicians.

Most of the teachers and support staff involved were not trained musicians. At first the task seemed daunting – having to learn an instrument alongside the class and being able to lead lessons teaching them new skills! It quickly became apparent that this was an ideal opportunity for teachers to

Linda, teaching assistant

I think staff have learnt a lot. Sometimes people think, there is no way I can do that. But you just look at the number of staff who play musical instruments now, loads of them. I mean some people are not particularly arty are they? I'm not but I'll have a go and I enjoy it. I mean I don't always get a great result but there is a fear isn't there? As a teacher or an adult in the class you feel that you have to show the kids that you're spot on, that you are an expert , but that's not the case. They like to see that we go wrong as well and that's good. I think so, I'm sure that's a good thing for the kids, to see we can't always be right – none of us.

Fiona, Newham Music Academy

During general musicianship lessons children develop rhythm, singing and notation skills as well as their ability to work together to create music.

Teachers in evaluation meetings

Sometimes the timetable wasn't flexible enough. We were still expected to cover all areas and keep up with assessment and that can be hard. However, the more practical activities have been fun for the children and the adults and given them an opportunity to acquire new skills.

implement some different learning and teaching styles as well as receive on the job training.

It was a big commitment by the class teachers, especially in terms of time – as it was, the curriculum was changing to incorporate the creative learning units and sometimes this seemed detrimental to other subjects. So to have to make an extra half hour at least each day seemed, at times, an impossible task. Despite this, it was an enjoyable and highly rewarding experience.

Impact on learning

Alongside the initial excitement (and sometimes panic), more serious questions were raised.

- How was this extra disruption to our school day and our curriculum going to ultimately benefit our pupils?
- How was it going to affect their learning across all areas of the curriculum?
- Were they going to enjoy it?
- What was important?
- Perhaps most importantly, could we do it?

I like music because you get to learn all kinds of music. *Year 4 pupil*

I like wider opportunities because you get to learn an instrument and not only that, you don't only learn notes and how things are played; we get to do it ourselves. *Year 6 pupil*

> In African drumming our teacher, every time we do it, says 'do it so you feel the rhythm of the music on your bodies'. It helps you learn how to be fluid with the music. *Year 5 pupil*

At first I was excited about having something new to teach and learn – and so were the children. When the staff and pupils got their first instruments, there was a lot of frustration that they were not magically transformed into virtuosi violin or recorder players! But, thanks to the professionalism of the visiting teachers and their ability to instil confidence in the children and staff, the frustration was soon replaced by 'Wow, we can play a recognisable tune'. It didn't seem to matter to them that they were only playing the same note repeatedly over a backing track! But they did sound good and with that self-belief and the growing confidence of the class teachers, who thought that they were 'non-musical', things started moving swiftly. Before we knew it, we were performing in concerts, not only at the school but at local venues. By the second year, our performances were receiving rapturous applause from audiences in the Royal Festival Hall and the Barbican; places that most of our children are unlikely ever to visit to listen to a concert, let alone perform on the stage! Their confidence soared – and still continues to grow.

The second year and onwards

In the second year of the project, it was decided that Year 3 children would benefit from a full year of General Musicianship lessons before learning an instrument. The previous Year 3 children continued to learn their instruments in Year 4. This required commitment from more teachers and support staff. Again, this was difficult with an already pressurised curriculum as well as our growing number of creative learning units. Nonetheless the enthusiasm continued.

At this point the schools became more involved with the forward planning of the project. We wanted to ensure that it continued to develop and was sustainable, so that children who already had two years of the programme would continue their musical journey in Years 5 and 6. Having been a class teacher in Year 3 and 4 for the previous two years, I took on the co-ordination of the project. We decided to give pupils the chance to try different instruments and to introduce more cultural diversity, in keeping with our community.

For the following year, the same format was followed in Years 3 and 4 and children in Year 5 were given a choice of one instrument for the entire year: so to continue with recorder or violin, or take up African Drumming or Samba.

Catherine, teacher artist

Although it was fantastic that pupils were able to have such a wide range of experiences it was very complex to organise. One of the original principles of Wider Opportunities was that once the pupils had experienced a period of time focused on learning to play one instrument they would be able to move on to learn an instrument of choice. It was impossible for us to give them a totally free choice so we negotiated a range of choices for the pupils to select from. Unfortunately for some pupils it was not possible for them to have their first choice immediately because some choices were oversubscribed. This meant that some pupils suffered a certain amount of disaffection.

Each was taught by visiting musicians. More emphasis was now placed on the children becoming responsible for their own practice. About a third of the original violin class chose to continue, which was very encouraging. In Year 6, the format was altered slightly to give the children not continuing with the recorder or violin a term's lessons each of Drumming, Samba and Vocals with Percussion. The idea was to enable the children to get a wider range of skills and experience and also help them to form opinions about what they do and don't like and why.

Our partner school decided that children would continue with their initial choice. Discussion with children and staff from both schools has shown the pros and cons of both systems. On the positive side, the children who continued with their initial choice have become very competent and, in the cases where they enjoy the instrument, are getting a lot out of it. On the negative, some children lost their initial enthusiasm with certain instruments.

Fitting in with our commitment to creative learning

So great! We know that the children's musical ability improved dramatically and they got fantastic opportunities but how does all this feed into their learning across the curriculum? How does it fit into our commitment to creative learning and teaching? Firstly, the children's increased confidence in their abilities allowed them to have a go more readily at activities they had

Tania, teacher

Their listening skills are very good and their general musicianship in terms of rhythm and pitch is better. They can manipulate their fingers in the way they want, which is quite a fine thing.

If I had done African drumming I would have learnt more about my culture and some other cultures and I think I would have learnt more because it would have been something I enjoyed. *Year 5 pupil*

Sue, parent

With the music side of things, I think it helps with their concentration. I think if they can concentrate on a piece of music then I think when they have a maths test they will be able to apply the same sorts of skill.

previously been wary of in other subjects. Teachers, and the children themselves, often reported that their listening skills improved. Increased concentration is also attributable in some way to their participation in Wider Opportunities.

During our creative journey it became apparent that we needed some way to create continuity and focus on learning in different ways, hence the key skills were introduced: evaluation, making links, meta learning and questioning. Later, these were joined by problem solving and personal communication. Throughout their music activities, the children developed their evaluation skills, as this aspect was built into most lessons. They were encouraged to identify how best they learn, and discussions helped some of them to transfer their meta learning skills to other areas of the curriculum. Some of the creative units undertaken throughout the school make links with music and other disciplines, and children can apply their musical learning in Design and Technology and Maths projects so it helps them deepen their understanding of the subjects.

Where do we go from here?

The Wider Opportunities project is now embedded in the curriculum in both schools. There are certainly downsides, not least the noise created in the fourteen different music lessons every Monday morning! But the pros, in my opinion at least, far outweigh the cons. The children perform regularly, both informally in assemblies and at concerts. We occasionally open our lessons to

I have learn that music can link to maths. If you have got the number of beats in a bar you can find out the ratio of how many beats on that stave. *Year 6 pupil*

In keyboards we learnt that if you play the middle c with your finger like this (displaying index finger) you are wrong and if you want to learn to play keyboards you cannot make your fingers lie like a stretching spider – you have to make them like running spiders legs. (displaying a hand with fingers pointing downwards) *Y4 pupil*

parents, who come and join in and learn alongside their children. This has proved to be a splendid opportunity to get parents into school to find out more about their children's learning. We have just had our school Summer Concert. This year it stretched to over an hour and a half because there was so much good practice to celebrate. It was attended by well over a hundred parents and carers, a fantastic turnout for our school, and they enjoyed it thoroughly. We also recently took a Samba band to play at Newham carnival. The children had only played together once before, yet with the skills and confidence they have amassed they pulled it off brilliantly. I feel immense pride in their achievements as do many other teachers and, of course, the children themselves and their families.

Children who might have gone through school without ever finding something they are good at have discovered they are musicians, and good ones at that. We recently had our first batch of children sit their Grade One violin exams, a fantastic achievement. One success story is about a child with challenging behaviour who encountered the violin in Year 3 and discovered that he was good at it. He then took to all forms of music, has just (in Year 6) done a solo performance in the Summer Concert and has started working with a local musician to produce his own tracks. Watch out for him in the future!

Now that the children who have been through this musical journey are beginning to leave Star, we are trying to create links with their secondary schools to ensure their talents are built on and not lost.

It is not only the children who have become more musically inclined but the staff too. Initially, it was only the teachers and support staff who taught

Catherine, teacher-artist

I think that one of the issues we are still trying to resolve is that of the pupils being creative with music. The pupils have learnt how to play instruments and read music and that has really boosted their confidence. We are still working on how we provide opportunities for pupils to use music creatively, to compose their own work using a range of sounds and in response to a range of stimuli.

classes who were learning violin or recorder who took up an instrument. Now however, we have an ever-growing staff violin group and at least three teachers have been inspired to rediscover instruments they had played as children. So this journey has been an enjoyable one and has formed bonds across our school communities and provided some unforgettable memories. Long may it continue!

Conclusion

Partnerships have been crucial to our development because we do not have all the expertise we need within the schools. Artists have a depth of knowledge and understanding of their art form which teachers are unlikely to have unless they have acquired it outside the school. We have learned a great deal about developing successful partnerships and the writing of the protocols provided both a summary of that learning and a guide for future work. Time and commitment are important factors in the success of partnerships and ensuring that the learning from each partnership can be embedded in both schools. The Wider Opportunities Scheme has also highlighted the importance of developing closer links with secondary schools to try and ensure that our pupils can, should they so choose, pursue their musical learning throughout their school careers.

Teri, headteacher

Drumming has had a profound effect on Zanda. Before he started, he was becoming disaffected with school and we were very worried about how he would manage when he transferred to secondary school. He has been transformed by realising that he is an able musician. Landing (the drumming teacher at Manor) told me that he has met several ex-pupils at secondary schools he's been working in recently. During a dance workshop last week, he saw Zanda and persuaded him to take the lead drumming part to accompany the dancers. Apparently, no-one knew he had this talent. We really need to do more to establish closer links with the arts departments in secondary schools.

4

PARTNERS' PERSPECTIVES
'I feel nervous because I'm going to have a new teacher that I don't know well'

This chapter reflects the perspectives of two of our partners: Stephen Mason, the dance artist who worked with us for a year and Martin Heaney, who was the researcher who tracked our development over four years.

My residency at Manor and Star – *Stephen Mason, Dance Artist*
After a successful collaboration between the creative learning programme in Manor and Star and myself during the autumn term 2003, a year long cross-curricular dance residency was established for the 2004-2005 academic year. I led the residency, supported by Corrie Lunghi, to work with all the Key Stage 2 classes in both schools, raising the profile and accessibility of dance as an art form within a cross-curricular framework. In Key Stage 1, I worked in partnership with a musician. By developing and evaluating units of work that contribute to the development of the creative learning curriculum, dance was used as a tool to:

- enhance pupils' knowledge and understanding of other curriculum areas
- support the principles of creative learning
- incorporate Howard Gardner's multiple intelligences theory (as described in *Frames of Mind*, 1983)
- support the development of the schools' key skills

Key Skills and Methodology

The dance sessions used the preferred framework for the teaching of dance in schools prescribed by the National Curriculum – Dance as Art model (Smith-Autard, 2002), whereby pupils compose, perform and appreciate dances – to ensure that the dance activities supported pupils in developing and engaging with the creative learning key skills: questioning, making links, meta-learning and evaluation. The Dance as Art model provides a range of opportunities for skill-based learning and problem-solving activities, so enabling pupils to develop and utilise their creativity. The three strands of the model require a range of activities to be included in every dance session for example:

> The work was quite impressive. When we were watching the video some bits of it were funny and some bits were interesting because you got to see how other people were getting on with their motifs.
>
> *Year 3 pupil*

Composing – making of dances	Performing – dancing and developing physical skills	viewing of dance
■ imagining	■ developing physical skill, poise, confidence	■ observing
■ researching	■ understanding intention, form and style	■ describing
■ exploring		■ recognising
■ improvising	■ sensitivity to other performers	■ reflecting
■ developing a dance vocabulary	■ developing accuracy and fluency	■ interpreting
■ problem-solving		■ comparing and contrasting
■ decision-making	■ practising	■ analysing
■ selecting	■ expressing	■ making judgements
	■ interpreting	■ evaluating
	■ refining	■ developing a critical language
	Appreciating – active	

(Descriptions selected and adapted from Arts Council, 1993, p6)

The Dance as Art model is an accessible and inclusive model for the facilitation of dance activities and learning through a variety of media. Sessions that use this model as a framework enable pupils to explore themes and ideas whilst drawing from and developing their own movement vocabulary. Movement content is derived from 'everyday movement and everyday descriptive words. This makes it possible for everyone to be able to create and perform

It made you feel nervous but when you done it you overcame your nerves... what I found hard was getting the whole dance together cause some people wanted to do something and some people were disagreeing and it's just like hard to work out... we just went alright we'll have your one for this but then we'll have our one for that.
Year 6 boy

dances immediately (Smith-Autard, 2002, p86) and does not rely on previous dance experience. The focus of this model in the Primary context provides an emphasis on the process, development of creativity and imagination, feelings and a problem-solving approach to learning (Smith-Autard, 2002, p196). Pupils are constantly required to solve problems and make connections between the movements they are creating, performing or watching and the subject they are representing. At every stage they need to evaluate their decisions or performance and engage in discussions, verbal or written, about their learning. At all times we referred to National Curriculum guidelines and QCA Physical Education Dance Schemes of Work were adapted to ensure that subject knowledge and content was appropriate for the pupils.

Learning styles, multiple intelligences, engaging pupils

When devising Units of Work and individual sessions I wanted to ensure that there was a clear 'focus on differing learning styles – visual, auditory and kinaesthetic' (Heaney and Shaw, 2004, p8). Although dance is a primarily physical activity, it is important to ensure that all learning styles are addressed in the session. Corrie and I explored a range of entry points and exploratory activities that sought to address every learning preference. Accordingly, we used a range of teaching strategies, each of which had a specific purpose:

- **Warm up sequences**: Warm up sequences prepared pupils both mentally and physically for the session: these were most effective if they were integral to the session and reflected the learning outcomes and stimulus of the lesson. These sections of the lesson formed a shared experience for pupils and created a supportive learning environment. Warm up exercises included performing shapes and movements that I would refer to or use later in the session or that pupils could use when creating their own dances. During warm ups pupils would make connections between the movements they were performing and subject knowledge. For example, in a session exploring India's cold climate, angular shapes were used to represent mountains and snowflakes, and fast, heavy movements to represent the monsoon season

■ **Movement-led games:** We used instructional movement-led games as an enjoyable introduction to a concept and to support further improvisations and tasks used in the session. They also helped pupils to start using key vocabulary and make links between the vocabulary and the movements. The concepts pupils have retained the most information about are those where games were used as an introduction to a new topic or concept. For example, in a session exploring the water cycle, pupils were given four instructions and responses to the key components of the cycle – evaporation, condensation, precipitation, water – and pupils called these out as they performed in response to the instruction

■ **Dance Artist and pupil demonstration (modeling) and set movement phrases:** This strategy combined teacher/class discussion, teacher demonstration of movement examples (firstly by Corrie or me and then by pupils) and class practice. Teachers frequently commented on this strategy as one that ensured all pupils could achieve in tasks and which provided examples of how concepts could be abstracted. It also allowed all learning styles to be addressed: the visual learners to watch, the aural to listen to my explanation about how the movement idea was created and physical learners to practice

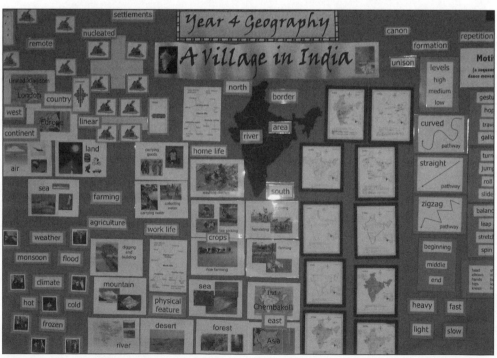

Year 4 notice board

- **Raps, mnemonics and word phrases:** These enabled pupils to acquire, retain and recall key vocabulary whilst addressing visual, aural and physical learners. We either devised them ourselves or took them from a CD-ROM teaching resource entitled *Science~Physical* (The Place, 2004). We gave pupils the simple word phrase *The ozone layer protects us from the sun's dangerous ultraviolet rays* and they created movements for each word underlined after playing a game that explored movement possibilities for each word. The movements were performed with the pupils calling out the word phrase to help them connect between physical, visual and aural activities

- **Notice boards and visual displays:** A notice board was used as a teaching aid. Flashcards with key vocabulary and supporting materials were placed on it then referred to throughout the dance sessions. Pupils would refer to the notice board at the beginning of sessions to remind them about the previous session, when completing movement tasks and answering questions. This enabled them to start developing the skills for becoming independent learners. The displays were a valuable resource for assisting pupils to make links between classroom and dance sessions

- **Movement Improvisation** enabled pupils to explore the stimulus of the session, develop dance skills and acquire a movement vocabulary they could draw on when completing tasks. Corrie or I generally guided the improvisations. Pupils had to problem-solve constantly, respond to a range of stimuli and evaluate their work.

- **Discussions** were integral to the sessions, requiring pupils to recall previous knowledge and understanding, use key vocabulary, pose and answer questions and make links   *S-AL*

- **Movement tasks** enabled pupils to continue to explore and consolidate the knowledge and understanding about a particular concept. Pupils problem-solved, collaborated and reflected with others and started to think and talk about their learning. For example, after exploring geographical settlements, the pupils explored travelling through the space. They had to stop four times, each time creating physical representations of settlements depicted on the flashcards we gave them.

- **Performing and evaluating dances** gave the pupils opportunities to present their knowledge and understanding and discuss their own work and that of others. Evaluation tasks required pupils to reflect, recall knowledge, make links and talk about their learning. Evaluat-

Year 4 discussion

ing also gave pupils an opportunity to watch and respond to the work of their peers. To enable pupils to make links and recognise the content of others performances I might ask pupils to call out what they saw. For example, at the end of a session exploring how magnets attract and repel, pupils were given a particular group to watch and asked to call out 'attract' or 'repel' to describe what the performers were representing

These strategies sought to meet all learning preferences. The Learning and Access department at The Place (London's National Dance Agency) describes as *multi-sensory approaches to learning* (The Place, 2004). We noticed that some sessions were more successful than others at incorporating a range of multi-sensory activities. Sessions that required significant knowledge acquisition hindered the multi-sensory experience, affecting the pupils' ability to explore and consolidate knowledge. As the residency progressed, we ensured that as much knowledge as possible was first acquired in the classroom to allow more time for exploration and consolidation of subject knowledge in the dance session.

Examples of Units of Work – key skills

The Year 3 Unit of Work – Magnets and Springs – was particularly successful in making links between classroom-based activities and dance sessions. It was also the unit that had the highest level of teacher participation. The content of the QCA Science Schemes of Work is clear and we easily translated it into movement sessions. Six sessions were delivered:

- forces: push and pull
- magnets and magnetic materials
- magnets: attraction and repulsion
- expanding springs
- compressing springs
- dance composition and performance session based on the above

The clarity of the content gave us additional time to plan class teacher input in the dance sessions. Links between classroom-based and dance sessions were made by teachers leading activities at the beginning or end of dance sessions in an attempt to support pupils in making links between the dif-

I really enjoyed it because we learnt a lot and even people who can't write properly like me, because we didn't have to write it down we just had to act it out. *Year 3 pupil*

> I think that dance and science is inspiring and it helps me to learn more about springs and magnets and how they work. I enjoyed it because we did different things every week. *Year 3 pupil*

ferent learning contexts. Before they had the Attraction and Repulsion dance session, pupils experimented with and discussed magnets in the classroom. After the warm up and rap that used the scientific vocabulary introduced during the scientific exploration, children created movements that represented the concepts and completed worksheets reflecting on the session. The session finished with the pupils responding to a computer programme linked up to the interactive whiteboard. They watched magnets attracting and repelling, identified the process and once again described the movements they had performed or watched in the dance.

> The roles of artists and teachers should therefore be seen in conjunction – the one relying on the other for the overall success of the scheme. (Calouste Gulbenkian Foundation, 1982, p120-121)

Most of the teachers embraced their roles in the sessions and actively participated in and contributed to the dance sessions. The pupils obviously enjoyed seeing their class teacher working with us. Where sessions began with a scientific exploration followed by a corresponding dance session we would refer back to the classroom-based activity. This helped the pupils to make links between the scientific exploration and the movements they were creating. Class teachers used our notice board for reference during their sessions and placed the pupils' work onto it to help them make links. Our observation of the class teachers allowed us to try out and evaluate new teaching strategies for leading class discussions and questioning pupils.

The Year 2 Unit of Work – Emotions – was also successful. It made links with classroom-based activities, primarily because one of the curriculum links was Literacy, which forms part of the day to day curriculum. The topic of Emotions was used as stimulus for most classroom activities for the three weeks. Because they had some prior knowledge of and thoughts about the stimulus for the session, the pupils were well prepared for the dance sessions and during them, class teachers supported discussions, reminding pupils of classroom-based work. For example the pupils, supported by the class teacher, identified the emotions described in a poem and discussed situations in which they had similar feelings. I asked pupils to respond to the following questions through movement improvisations: What level might you

Linda, teaching assistant

.... when I think about the dance and movement that we did with Stephen you could just see the kids flourish, I mean all the pupils with special needs and with English language needs, because language doesn't matter when you're doing art. That's the way I see it.

The dance was forces and magnets, and the kids that normally wouldn't get it from the textbook or even from ICT... take it on board but with the dance there is that physical contact. I mean Cyril, who had special needs, teamed up with another child and the movements they made were really good and he knew all about the north pole and the south pole attracting and repelling. He wouldn't have got that sitting on the carpet listening or looking at the white board because he tends to go off.... when they are taking part and being active they learn better... when they came back to class we made a book, I was amazed at what they had learnt. Cyril would never take part in a PE lesson before, he never liked the contact, he would stand back, but this year it has been amazing that he really took part. I don't really have any idea why he has changed. He never used to like the contact he didn't like having to get undressed and we had tears in the beginning, apparently he has always been like that. I didn't really know him before this year; now he's ready to join in. It is quite fun. It's not just him, I mean, it's the other children in the class as well but it has been very significant for Cyril.

travel on when feeling that emotion? What size would the movement be? I asked them to select a movement from the warm up that they thought best represented the emotion, to discuss their choices and choose the most appropriate to represent the emotion to perform for a partner.

The teachers enjoyed and valued the dance sessions as an activity that enhanced pupils' understanding of the emotions. Teachers used them as a stimulus for developing the pupils' vocabulary for discussing emotions. One teacher identified language development as a particular benefit: the pupils' written work showed significant use of associated vocabulary. I believe these outcomes were only possible because of the class teachers' active participation and willingness to take responsibility for their contribution to the unit.

The Year 4 unit of work – A Village in India: Chembakoli – was the most successful in terms of the range of strategies and activities used in the sessions

Emma, teacher
Stephen was fantastic. From Stephen I learned alongside the pupils.

A pupil's notations on movement related to different kinds of travel.

catering for all learning preferences – visual, auditory and kinaesthetic. This was one of our favourite units of work because it went beyond the obvious in terms of what dance explored – a range of content relating to India and not just Indian dance – and used a significant variety of resources and strategies to ensure that all the pupils were given an understanding of the cultures involved. A particularly successful session explored geographical settlements. Pupils arranged houses on a notice board to show different settlements and then identified the settlement they live in and the settlement that best described Chembakoli. These visual descriptions were then used as the framework for a game in which the pupils moved around the space and created a physical representation of the settlement I called out. We kept referring back to the notice board so the pupils would connect the name of the settlement with the visual and physical representations.

This led into a movement task: pupils were asked to travel through the space in small groups and create more elaborate physical representations of different settlements, responding to set criteria. We gave each group little flashcards to help them remember the settlements and they had the notice board to refer to. The class teachers rated this session as extremely successful. It was one of the pupils' favourites and it was the first time for most pupils in each class that they understood the complex terms. At the end of the session the

Giraffes Can't Dance

This excerpt from a conversation with Donna and Razia, Nursery teacher and nursery nurse, illustrates some of the ways the partnership with Stephen affected the pupils and staff.

Donna: Stephen – he was amazing. I thought there is no way you are getting me up there dancing, no way on this earth, but I did. We repeated the unit ourselves this year. We loved it. We followed his plan because it was such a good lesson plan; it was absolutely fantastic. I really enjoyed myself.

Razia: The children really took to it as well.

Donna. This year we linked it with a trip to Colchester Zoo. We did a huge display on a jungle theme, we went to the zoo, we did dance, we had photographs up on the interactive white board and we did a lot of art activities and even now, some months later they still talk about the giraffes and the zoo. We have just been to Legoland and there was nowhere near as much enthusiasm.

Razia: With the puppets and the dance their vocabulary really developed. Where often there are children who would just come in and play and be unwilling to talk, they were all talking and coming up with really good ideas.

Donna: It really took us aback.

Razia: They really got into it – the book and the dance

Donna: When they were doing the dance they were relating it to their own experience at the zoo because they were allowed to feed Gerald the Giraffe. So they were all saying 'I saw Gerald at the Zoo.' Or 'I fed Gerald.' It was brilliant.

Razia: Yes they were able to remember and we put all their ideas in a book like 'Giraffes can't dance'.

Donna: I remembered when we were doing that dance one of the parents came up to me the next day and asked if we had been doing dance. Apparently her son had insisted on showing her in the street. They picked his brother up and he refused to move until he had shown her the dance he had just done. He said, 'I'm Gerald and this is how I walk,' and he showed his Mum on the pavement. Then he said, 'this is his neck and he had wobbly legs,' and he actually rolled on the pavement. His mum said we couldn't go home till he had shown me. I thought that was lovely.

Donna: When we did it last year with Stephen we chose to work with just the older children in nursery but this year we got all the children involved. We did it in small groups and we thought we might have to adapt it for the different groups but we didn't need to. They were so interested and because it was physical and they could come up with their own ideas, even the younger ones who are only three coped really as well as the four year olds. Whereas last year we were a bit worried that the younger ones wouldn't manage.

Razia: I think partly it was that we took them outside into the hall and we had them in a circle and they had to take off their shoes and socks and put the music on.

Giraffes Can't Dance (continued)

Donna: You do have to warn them what we are going to do that we will need to take their shoes off because we are going out to a different space. They are going out of their known environment. They coped really well.

Donna: It's made me like dance basically. I just didn't have the confidence before because I didn't know much about it and I thought I would look an idiot doing it.

Razia: Well Stephen was a very good role model.

---

pupils documented in any way they wanted – generally through drawings or diagrams – their understanding of the session. Most were able to draw a diagram of the settlement, their movements that represented the settlement and to label it using technical dance and subject vocabulary. The notice board was integral to each session and flashcards and pictures of key concepts were posted onto it. Teachers identified the resources used and created by us as a strength of this unit.

Partnership, Research and Teacher Enquiry – *Martin Heaney*

Manor Star Partnership – Moving into Action Research Phase 3

We had the chance to test the aims, objectives and delivery of A+, by extracting 'hard' data and presenting a focused research model in just two schools in the Education Action Zone (Manor and Star).

The scale of this made the action research more robust and achievable on a longitudinal basis and increased the opportunity for exchanges between partners.

The model worked on Action Research Methodology, with collaboration between project managers, teachers, teaching assistants, artists, arts organisations, pupils, headteachers and governors at its centre. The research fed directly and constantly into the shape, design and content of the programme. We used the PARAPET model: Participatory Action Research for the Advancement of Practice in Education and Teaching, a critical framework which focuses on social justice through partnership and promotes parity between the researcher and those being researched.

Andi, Director SW Newham EAZ

As a researcher for the A+ Programme (creative learning) from 2002-2005, I worked with Pam Shaw, from the Central School of Speech and Drama, documenting and evaluating the effects of the implementation of the A+ Programme in Manor and Star Primary Schools. The process, and the final report for the Gulbenkian Foundation in 2004, followed a traditional academic model: observing teacher-artist collaborations and pupil work, with interviews before and after the process to create data about pupil progress and changes in teachers' attitudes. The report noted considerable advances in the partnership schools in extending the debate on learning and creativity – with wider participation by teachers in reforming arts-led curricula. The effects of implementation and the rapid embedding of changed practices and systems had been unpredictable and tested the premises and methodology initiated by the research team. The need for adaptability to changing systems became apparent early in the research journey. The role of 'traditional' academic research in a fast-evolving programme of lateral school reform is discussed in this chapter. It explores some of the opportunities and challenges that arise when developing new partnerships between schools and academic researchers.

The Final Report of Phase 3 of the A+ Programme (2002-2004) had documented strong connections between pupils' perceptions of learning well and enjoyment in the arts (Heaney and Shaw, 2004). Particular gains were noted by pupils with special educational needs and English as an additional language throughout the programme. Other models of quantitative data analysis were employed to co-relate improvements with Standard Assessment Test (SATs) results, but these were problematic. Richer data had emerged in tracking the debate within the Partnership schools about the direction of the programme. The process of debate around the A+ philosophy and principles played a key part in programme delivery. Recognising that the dialogue on learning was itself transformative, we wanted to document this debate and its impact. Some significant elements of the debate featured in the Final Report to the Gulbenkian Foundation including:

- the interrogation of the relationship between the arts and learning, which produced significant working papers within the Partnership
- the debate and documentation of Inset on the perceived tension between implementing the new curricular model and the National Curriculum
- the creation of a new protocol (produced by school staff in collaboration with an artist in residence) for future collaborations.

The next phase of the A+ (now creative learning) Programme in late 2004, with direct funding from the DfES Innovations Unit for the development of a new approach to Continuing Professional Development (CPD) and funding for the next phase of research, brought further development in the dialogue between stakeholders and, with it, new challenges in a reconsideration of the relationship between teachers and research. Key focuses of the next phase to be tracked by the research team included developing devolved leadership and the Connecting Conversations process – plus in-service education (Inset) to enable teachers to become researchers of effective practice, which I facilitated. The goal was to embed the successful practices of creative learning in a more democratic model.

The new strategy began with a period of open debate about the merits and purposes of previous research. At an Inset discussion about findings of the Final Report, staff identified significant advances in embedding the new creative learning curriculum and acknowledged that the new model still had deficits, for example, in parent involvement and child-led activity. The academic style of the report was criticised for being rather inaccessible. Some teachers thought that the focus on studies of certain year groups had excluded other year groups from the researchers' attention. The Final Report had both reflected and stimulated debate.

At issue here, I believe, is the relevance of research activity to the processes of school reform. In the previous research period, significant gains had been documented in observations of specific year group work and more anecdotal evidence indicated that teacher-researcher dialogue was also stimulating the debate on learning – but limitations of scale had prohibited wider engagement between researchers and teachers. The next stage of research needed to involve more teachers more deeply.

It is important at this point to acknowledge also that a significant impetus for broadening participation in research came not just from the schools themselves but through a Department for Education and Skills drive to promote evidence-informed practice. Debate around these policies and capacity-building in schools raises many questions for researchers in relation to participation in research and the dissemination of data.

Hargreaves' argument that the shift from driving up standards in literacy and numeracy to longer-term transformation requires deeper reform 'stimulating disciplined processes of innovation within the school system, and building an infrastructure capable of transferring ideas, knowledge and new practices laterally across it (Hargreaves, 2003),' is helpful. Arguably, many recent UK

Catherine, teacher-artist

In a sense, the planning processes and structures we developed are, in themselves, research. We have been working in new ways and evaluating continuously and those evaluations, whilst not public, are opportunities to share our learning.

research projects in the arts and creative learning have been preoccupied with demonstrating, through detailed impact analyses, the usefulness of the arts in driving up standards in 'core' subjects. However, if the agenda is changing away from driving up standards in literacy and numeracy, as Hargreaves asserts, is it appropriate for arts-based researchers to continue to keep trying try to demonstrate the value of the arts in relation to the 'core' subjects agenda? If genuine transformation of learning is the goal of school reform why continue to pursue research questions if they do not immediately relate to practitioner empowerment and transformation at grass roots level?

These questions are complex but they represent dilemmas that go to the heart of research activity in schools. The pressure to collate 'hard' data to demonstrate to funders and policy-makers the impact of the arts on learning was intense throughout the previous research programme. At the same time, the transformations that had already occurred created their own momentum for change and a demand for a much wider exchange of ideas than was possible with previous methods of research. Funding from the DfES Innovations Unit created an opportunity in 2004 to link research activity more effectively to the capacity-building agenda.

Teacher enquiry

The strategic decision to engage teachers with research opened up new possibilities to broaden the research base in the schools partnership. At the Inset event to discuss Final report findings, there were exercises for teachers to identify their own research questions as a springboard for the next phase. Six teachers voluntarily took their questions forward in a process that I facilitated and supported. There was much discussion about the appropriate definition for this activity, some preferring 'teacher enquiry' to 'teacher research'. This reflected some uncertainty about the final outcomes of the teachers' work in terms of dissemination and a desire to raise the status of the activity to 're-search' i.e. to publish the results of the investigation.

All the research interviews demonstrated the practitioners' keen involvement in identifying research questions and appropriate methodology. At the end of

Group questions following research Inset 2004

How can we make the project more child-centred and less teacher led?

How can we make our approach more child-centred?

How can it place the children at the centre of learning? How can we develop all children's responsibility for and control over their learning?

How can creative learning address the increasing gap between enjoyment of 'arts based' projects and learning and growing reluctance towards boring subjects like reading, writing, spelling and certain numeracy topics?

How will basic skills – reading, writing and spelling – be developed through creative learning projects?

How do we get the balance between workload, academic achievement and the arts to create an all round balanced individual?

How can we incorporate creative learning into raising attainment in the core subjects?

Is creative learning sustainable over the whole year for every year group – so that all things are taught through the arts?

Children as researchers – can we act on what our research has revealed?

How can we recognise or measure what the children are learning besides their academic achievement?

How can we monitor and record individual progress across the year groups, focusing on special educational needs?

In planning, how can we differentiate effectively in order to develop pupils' interpersonal skills to enable them to become facilitators?

How can we keep the quality of the partnership for staff and children – such as personal interaction, sharing ideas, bonding – as the partnership is expanding and branching out?

How can we include parents in a structured way and use their expertise in the classroom and with staff?

How can we make all staff feel that they are valued and not be made to feel that children's progress is due to creative learning and not their hard work, enthusiasm and commitment to children's learning?

the project, practitioners had collected their own data of children's involvement in creative learning or submitted their findings orally in interview.

However, my expectations of the production of written papers were unrealistic for several reasons: some teachers lacked the confidence to share written work, two of the participants could not complete their projects for personal reasons. A far greater challenge was posed by the introduction of preparation, planning and assessment (PPA) time, which consumed time that teachers had allocated for their work. The creation of the conditions – by researchers and school leaders – for immediate dissemination to colleagues through a shared evaluation of individual projects, Inset and ultimately, a contribution to a local network conference for teacher researchers created an effective alternative way to make the results of teacher enquiries 'public'.

Teachers at research evaluation meeting

What is research?
- questioning
- child centred
- evidence and outcome
- challenging ideas and concepts
- a process of evaluation with constant reflection, moving on and changing
- investigating, questioning, tracking
- reporting and challenging previous ideas
- involving all pupils
- exploring teaching strategies
- constant assessment
- observation

> *Tula, teacher*
>
> This process has impacted on my professional development. I have learnt that more learning can take place when the child is allowed to explore in their own ways, even if they are unconventional. I have always been a strong believer in independent learning but have learnt more about when to withdraw and the importance of it.

As part of the shared evaluation, all participants discussed their conception of 'research' in relation to their projects. This discussion established that although 'enquiry' has been adopted in the two schools as a more user-friendly term than 'research', all practitioners identified investigating, tracking, assessment and observation as key components of both teaching practice and research. 'Research' was not viewed as an alien or 'academic' term. Conceptualisations of research went far beyond data gathering to a much wider synthesis of concepts and evidence from a range of disciplines (Saunders, 2004).

Practitioners also evaluated the usefulness of the strategies they had used and the most successful for maximising the potential of teacher observation: finding time to write down and reflect on observations, planning in more team-teaching opportunities to allow for observations and making greater use of 'instant' data capture, e.g. with Polaroid and digital cameras (see the creative learning website). In these evaluative discussions, my role changed from researcher to facilitator, inviting discussion of methodology and reflection on data produced and guiding participants towards critical assessment of their work. At the same time, the evaluation was informed by the needs and objectives of the participants. All identified that their research/enquiry and evaluative discussions were beneficial to their practice.

The process of A+ / creative learning practitioner research outlined thus far is consistent with the concept of 'engagement with research' (National Teacher Research Panel 2005). The NTRP study and other recent comparative reviews of teacher research (eg Simons *et al*, 2003), highlight the considerable differences in perceptions and approaches to research among practitioner groups. Simons identifies the improvement of practice as a key goal for teachers in engaging with research, where research findings are 'situationally-bounded' rather than linked to a wider body of theory or other studies.

The creative learning teacher enquiry provided insights into how the teachers related to research. They clearly had a working conceptual understanding of how different aspects of research related to their practice but they found writing up their findings more challenging. A local conference on building evidence-informed practice offered a welcome opportunity to share practice informally with professionals from similar working contexts and gave practitioners an incentive to prepare presentations based on their work.

The conference, described on the creative learning website, identified some common obstacles for practitioners in developing evidence-informed practice, such as the need to secure enough school time and leadership support before starting their research. Teacher researchers from various working groups observed that teacher enquiry may produce evidence that is difficult to deal with institutionally and professionally. Schools and researchers need to create space to deal with such eventualities.

Summary

What are the lessons for other partnerships between schools and researchers? Teachers were clear that the opportunity to observe was fundamental to the success of their enquiries and that adequate time and leadership support was essential. Frameworks need to be secure, based on contractual agreement at the outset to deal with problematic information. Achieving clarity on different models of research and particularly the articulation of a clear distinction between teacher enquiry and teacher research might have given more focus to determining outcomes. The dialogue between researchers and teacher practitioners about what counts as research was nevertheless transformative.

We learned to recognise different expectations and approaches to research activity. Theoretical perspectives of 'engagement with research' and the importance of 'situationally-bound knowledge' (Simons 2003) were important guides for me in examining my own expectations of outcomes. The primary commitment to improving practice was embedded at all levels of teacher enquiry. My challenge, as researcher and facilitator, was to support the

Andi, Director SW Newham EAZ

...another key outcome for me has been the way in which the teachers have become researchers and have used the findings of their action research to inform their own learning. They have applied their learning to a wide range of contexts.

teachers in finding a channel to share the outcomes of their enquiries. Presenting to their peers was an alternative to publication that they found more comfortable. Local networking is conducive to schools-based research and enquiry – but it challenges the traditional model of academic research where papers are published in academic journals. New models of partnership research require some delicate negotiation over the ultimate purposes of the work and the choice of platform to share findings. The relationship of the academic researcher to the site of research must change so that the relevance of research findings is evident to the school 'host'. The agenda has to shift from traditional 'dissemination' to 'transformation' (Saunders 2004).

In the new relationship, researchers assume a facilitative role guiding practitioners in their own research journey. A facilitative model of this kind does not assume knowledge of teachers' learning or experience or impose traditional models of research 'absolutes'. In a partnership model, the research facilitator seeks to energise and sustain the engagement of practitioners, proposing the agenda and seeking to encourage their commitment to sharing their findings with others.

There are tensions within research partnerships between academic models, where rigorous data analysis and publication are regarded as essential, and developmental models, where improving practice is prioritised. I do not claim this case study is a model of ideal practice but it certainly helped us to consider possible developments in democratic research partnerships in school communities.

Teri, headteacher

Having a researcher involved in observing, and reflecting back to us, aspects of our day-to-day work has been truly illuminating. We make so many assumptions about what we do and why we do it. Having someone probe our methodology has made us think more clearly and deeply. Staff in the year groups where Martin has focused have spoken time and again about the impact this had on their practice. It is a phenomenon of ethnographic research – and one we discussed in steering group meetings. However, I think this is a difficulty for researchers but is to our advantage. From my point of view, the process has two major advantages. Firstly, we get an honest, dispassionate view of the impact of what we are doing. Secondly, the process of engaging with a researcher makes us think more clearly and discuss at a deeper level the ways in which we can learn and improve.

Acknowledging the 'situated knowledge' and the demand for local dis-semination proved more relevant and useful than committing to a written outcome. The possibilities of dissemination in local networks and through the Internet have also created valid platforms for flexible communication. To achieve a truly transformative model of research, the relationship between researchers and schools has to become a genuine partnership (National Teacher Research Panel 2004) in which what counts as 'research' or 'evidence' is resolved in philosophical discussions. This dialogic approach, fundamental to building a community of practice, fosters genuine transformation by ack-nowledging the different interests and perspectives on research and the determination of all the participants.

Conclusion

This chapter highlights the huge potential of partnerships with artists in inspiring all school staff and giving them the tools and resources to develop their own practice. It demonstrates that the experiential nature of arts related learning has the potential to engage all learners and support them in developing their understanding of complex concepts.

In addition, our partnership with researchers promoted some deep thinking by teachers into the concept of research itself and the identification of the reflective processes they engage in every day.

5

CONTINUING PROFESSIONAL DEVELOPMENT

'I am developing the confidence to have a go'

This section, which starts by quoting a teaching assistant, is about teachers and support staff and their learning during the project. Teacher Violet Otieno, and teacher-artist Cathcrine McGill describe the processes developed, some of the training sessions offered and evaluate their effectiveness. Andi Smith explains the impact on his own practice. Teri N'Guessan describes the role of the teacher artist and its impact on staff development.

Continuing professional development
– Violet Otieno and Catherine McGill

Continuing professional development means developing and improving the quality of your work. Professional learning can take place in a wide range of formal and informal contexts. We believe that the best model of CPD is that which has a sustained impact on learning and teaching. As the DfES states: 'The strength of a profession resides in the capacity of its members to challenge, test and develop the knowledge and understanding on which its practice is based' (DfES, 1995-2004).

Lucy and Violet, teachers

The Insets and workshops we have attended, especially where we chose the area of development ourselves, have been very helpful – like drama and dance. It has helped us feel more confident in delivering lessons for pupils and supporting their learning.

Some Insets have not met our expectations, like the West Ham Conference. That time could have been used more effectively.

> *Tania, teacher*
>
> Most of the specific CPD was useful, for example art and painting. I actually learnt a lot from participating in artist-led sessions because I was seeing the use in practice.

The creative learning partnership between Manor and Star schools has offered teachers and teaching assistants a variety of CPD opportunities; they have ranged from workshops to differentiated staff meetings, discussions and opportunities for teacher research. There is also a system in place for teachers to discuss, plan and team-teach with the permanent teacher-artist and teachers in the partner school.

To introduce all staff to the principles, practice and structure of the project, the steering group devised the initial two-days programme described more fully in Chapter 1.

One of Catherine's roles in those first sessions included asking staff to identify their strengths within the arts, so that future CPD opportunities would meet the perceived needs of the participants. She collated that information and, in discussion with the heads and co-ordinators from each school, devised a further three days training for the beginning of the spring term, three half days of which would be devoted to the visual arts.

But we knew that the teachers had all had extensive Inset on preferred learning styles whereas the support staff had not. So we decided that in order to ensure that all staff had a common starting point the support staff would have some separate sessions during those three days, focused on developing their understanding of learning styles and the impact these might have on their own work in relation to children's learning.

In response to the teachers' survey we decided the teachers would focus on three-dimensional work and printing. A significant number of teachers and

> *Linda, teaching assistant*
>
> Some of the training days we've had I thought 'Oh no – that's too much' but we needed it because you have to have someone to give you an example... What has been the hardest for me, and I know it's the same for a lot of people, teachers as well, is when all the top people were there and they were using language that put them up there above us and everybody else was at a loss – I didn't actually know what they were talking about ...

support staff had no experience of using galleries as a resource and felt insecure about planning visits. So we set aside one half day for three-dimensional work, another for printing and photography, and arranged to take all the staff to Tate Modern for a semi-structured visit.

Andi, Director SW Newham EAZ

Support staff programme

To consider

- the implications of current research around Preferred Learning Styles and the relevance of this research in the classroom

- approaches to planning and classroom management that help all pupils to achieve

- a style of teaching for *All Our Futures*

Opportunities were provided that enabled participants to experience learning through a range of physical, visual and auditory activities. The programme culminated in a demonstration lesson, using a short story, 'The Party', as the stimulus. The story was read and then explored using Still Picture, Pupil in Role, Hot Seating, Body Print, Spontaneous Improvisation, Forum Theatre, Thought Tracking and Caption. Each group wrote a collective poem and analysed the processes they had engaged with in relation to their preferred learning style. The story was then explored through movement, focusing on grammar and the use of verbs. Each group did a presentation of the short story that included the use of drama, dance and the spoken word, including their poetry. All agreed that although each group's presentation focused on different aspects of the story, they were all equally powerful. Some felt the poetry should be published.

Evaluation of support staff training

The vast majority of the participants showed a commendable commitment to the education of all pupils. Many said they were working as teaching assistants because they wanted to make a difference and because of their personal experiences at school. Some said they were particularly committed because their own children had found school difficult and had clearly not been given the support one would expect.

The biggest concern for most seemed to be how their teaching colleagues would be applying the principles of preferred learning styles in the classroom. Many felt it was not clearly identified within the lesson planning. Marion, a head teacher who was present for the concluding session, reassured participants that all teaching staff had followed similar training and would be working within the framework for their planning and delivery. Several projects were then cited as examples of how preferred learning styles were already being addressed.

We wanted the participants to have experiences that not only provided new ideas for work in the classroom but also gave them an opportunity to work at their own level. We therefore organised several workshops to run simul-taneously, using the expertise already available amongst the staff and two artists who specialise in printing. The visit to Tate Modern was structured so that we utilised the understanding and expertise of staff who felt able to lead small group discussions about a few pre-selected artworks. We had a pre-liminary meeting at the Tate with this group to identify artworks and consider questions and strategies they might use to stimulate discussion.

The main objectives for the second three-day event were

- to build a CPD programme that took into account staff evaluations and comments from the initial two day event
- to continue to embed the culture of creative learning among the staff of Manor and Star schools
- to promote a community of shared learning
- to take into account the well being of staff
- to investigate aspects of Emotional Intelligence within a curricular framework

Practical workshops focused on developing photography, printing, three-dimensional work and activities related to sculpture.

To maximise the workshops' value, staff were asked to grade which ones would be most useful for them and Catherine arranged the groups accord-ingly. Although this was time consuming and balancing the numbers was tricky, it was well worth the effort because it was ultimately motivating.

Teacher

During one of the workshops when I had the chance to try different things out like photography... by participating I learnt that by making mistakes I can learn from them.

Content and delivery

A variety of learning strategies and styles were used to convey the speakers' and artists' aims and intentions. We wanted to model the approach to learning we were promoting for use in the classroom. This was achieved through interactive workshops, led predominately by teaching staff from both schools, visiting artists and staff from the Education Action Zone and Newham's advisory service.

On the first two morning sessions, the staff, in four groups, all covered the following: independent research activities, emotional intelligence, yoga and visualisation, massage.

The first afternoon session focused on the exploration and creation of three dimensional work through a variety of skills-based workshops. These included opportunities for staff to consider how the activity affected them, how it could be incorporated into their classroom practice and what benefits the pupils might derive from it.

On the second afternoon, the teaching and support staff visited the Tate Modern, the intention being to develop strategies for posing critical questions relating to art works. Some people expressed reservations about this visit on the grounds that they did not like modern art.

The third day's practical input was focused on explorations of printmaking, photography and digital imaging. Staff could also choose to continue to explore media from the first day's input.

Overall evaluation of second three days

The main points that arose from the evaluations of the arts input were that

■ the overall level of satisfaction was very good
■ most teachers felt that the workshops gave them opportunities to consider the relationship between the arts and learning
■ both support staff and teachers raised concerns about a lack of cohesion because they had had different experiences

Petra, teacher

I feel I have developed a far better understanding of how people learn. Moving from learning styles to multiple intelligences to the development of key skills has made me focus on the learning process.

Developing our own art skills through Inset has often been enjoyable and has certainly made me reflect on the process we expect children to go through.

Violet, teacher

At the very beginning of the project there were a series of whole day in service training events, designed to introduce creative learning and share effective practice. Advisors from the borough offered guidance through specific lesson ideas and more general philosophy about creative learning and teaching. The feedback from staff at this time was highly positive; with many people feeling encouraged and motivated by a different model of working which appeared to be more flexible and exciting – certainly compared to those National Literacy Strategy videos from the DfES!

- most teachers found the practical sessions of great value, and wanted 'more of the same'. They felt they had benefitted from the opportunity to work at their own level and with an 'expert'.

- some staff found the trip to the Tate challenging and had some difficulty with seeing how they might apply the experience; others found it enlightening and have gone on to organise their own visits

- some felt that application of the various processes in the classroom would be challenging

Outcome of the evaluation

Discussion about all the evaluations led us to conclude that we needed to

- continue to develop a CPD programme across the two schools based on a needs assessment of the learners. We felt this would develop the partnerships already being established, as well as providing targeted workshops that extend participants' skills, knowledge and understanding in the arts

- ensure there would be further opportunities to secure knowledge and understanding of cross-curricular planning, monitoring and evaluating arts processes

- develop a schedule for monitoring the impact of CPD through lesson observation

Andi, principal manager of professional development and EAZ director

I think my own personal learning has impacted significantly on my current role of Principal Manager of Professional Development, also in my other role as director of the SW Newham EAZ. When you are engaged in a dialogue about learning you can't help but transfer key elements of your learning to the other contexts in which you are working. For instance, in my role as manager of CPD I have been able to develop a debate about learning at my management level. I don't think that has been done before. Prior to that it was about the functionality of the service and the delivery. That still goes on, but we are engaging our advisory senior managers and our own CPD team in a debate about how we see ourselves as learners and what value can we add to the service to impact on others learning. We are thinking about what do we need to create other learning situations. That is something else which has come out of the project – how do staff not only teach subjects but coach and mentor their peers to become better learners? How do we create an organisation that promotes more integrated learning? I have taken the structure created by this partnership into the CPD service.

- continue to build aspects which challenge teachers and support staff's perceptions of the arts and learning into the CPD map
- ensure that support staff are encouraged to contribute their knowledge and understanding to teaching and learning
- establish a common language that can express the partnership of the arts and learning working as one
- continue to build on the structuring of questions to determine specific intentions and outcomes
- give year groups greater opportunity to plan collaboratively
- ensure that training would in the future include all staff, so that a shared dialogue and common purpose could be developed.

Subsequent observation in the schools suggested that the programme had significant impact on the teaching and learning. There is far greater awareness and sensitivity to different genres of visual art. Discussions about learning are more frequent and more informed and there are more visits to galleries by both staff and pupils.

The success of this programme depended heavily on being able to provide opportunities that met the perceived needs of the participants as well as those identified by the steering group. So we continued to provide training opportunities that responded to surveys and needs analysis. We focused on four areas:

> *Teacher*
>
> The drama was too practical and was all stuff that I have seen and a lot I had used before. I felt more time should have been spent on how to actually implement and execute the creative learning project.

- developing the capacity to make links between the arts and other curriculum areas
- developing a model for learning and teaching
- developing skills related to arts processes and identifying how they relate to skills across the curriculum
- developing understanding of the development of multiple intelligence and its role in learning and teaching

The Insets offered were significantly embedded in both schools' Improvement Plans. This means that the leadership of the two schools had collaborated and agreed priorities in terms of the partnership. The creative learning team met on a regular basis to plan, discuss, reflect and evaluate the developments. These meetings provided opportunities for representatives from both schools to question and plan future training events and to contribute to strategic plans that met the needs of the staff and would impact on learning and teaching. As a result the schools developed a clear overview and strategic plan.

The most obvious opportunity to affect learning and teaching was the year group units planned with the teacher-artist. The emphasis was on cross-curricular links and how learning in an art form can enhance learning across other subjects. The units were team planned, team taught and team evaluated along with the teacher-artist and teachers from both schools, allowing skills and expertise to be shared. This model has been continued throughout the project, involving other specialists such as Stephen, the dancer in residence.

As the partnership evolved, this model continued, but with less direct input from the teacher-artist. The idea is to achieve sustainability, with teachers taking more ownership and supporting other teachers in the year group. Over time as the two schools have embedded their learning into systems and structures appropriate to their own settings, less time is spent on joint sessions. We continue to try and provide a range of opportunities for development – practical and theoretical, self-chosen and directed, differentiated and whole staff.

Teachers' feedback

Weaving workshop

Interesting session enjoyed it – good use of materials and resources, well planned. There could have been more explanation on outcomes. Would have liked more ideas of how to teach this to my five year olds.

Felt making

An excellent Inset, just right, with background information, demonstration and practical activity. Would have been great if we had more information on prices for a whole class

I really enjoyed the session would love to try this with the whole class, very inclusive

I really enjoyed the workshops, a creative open-ended activity which can be differentiated for all children. It would be good to have further ideas.

Starch resist workshop session

A very practical session, can easily be used in the classroom, good link to the village in Africa Year 4. The kids would love it.

Music

Following through the needs analysis and our involvement in the Wider Opportunities Pilot, teachers identified their lack of confidence and musical knowledge as a problem for developing music creatively in their classrooms. We worked with the Newham Academy of Music, a music Advanced Skills Teacher and a musician from the Guildhall Connect project to try and provide a range of experiences for people to select from. Each member of staff could select two of the following to take part in:

- singing
- Kodaly – a system for developing understanding of musical notation
- literacy and music links
- composition/improvisation

The evaluation revealed the varied experience of the participants. Most found the warm up for the day, done by the whole group together, energising, fun and non-threatening while also useful for developing their classroom practice. Responses to the subsequent sessions ranged widely. Some groups felt they had learnt a great deal about making curriculum links with music, and developed the confidence and motivation to try out new ideas in their classroom. Others felt that although they had enjoyed the day their understanding

> *Teacher*
>
> I didn't really feel I got a lot from it, there wasn't much I felt I could use back in school.

had not progressed because there was no differentiation. A few were more confused by the end of the day than they were at the beginning.

When asked to identify the next steps for themselves, the replies again varied. Some wanted the opportunity to develop their own skills at a personal level, by learning an instrument or joining a choir. Others wanted Inset opportunities to develop their knowledge and understanding at their own level. This echoes the comments about differentiation. Several participants said they had enjoyed the day but had learned nothing new because the sessions were inadequately differentiated to meet their individual needs.

What we learned from the evaluation influenced the planning of future Inset. When planning the music day we had addressed the broad content of the sessions but had failed to describe them clearly enough for people to be able to differentiate for themselves and identify which sessions they would find most useful. We had not been involved in the planning of the actual sessions with the providers and realised that if we had, we could have helped the staff to make informed choices about which sessions to attend. All this led us to consider how we might differentiate more accurately in providing challenging, high quality and appropriate experiences for all staff.

> *Klara, Graduate teacher programme student*
>
> I was very nervous before the induction sessions, especially the first one, because I didn't know what to expect and I am not very good at arts. I thought I wouldn't be able to take part in the sessions properly but I was amazed at how well they went and how much I gained from them. I realised how important it is to incorporate creative learning into the teaching of all subjects and how much fun the children have learning in that way. I had no idea it was possible to teach so many different subjects through drama, music, dance and art. The sessions equipped us with a lot of very useful and practical ideas to use in our year groups.
>
> *Student*
>
> There was far too much information packed into the first session. I didn't have time to take it all in and came away feeling rather lost.

Developing an induction and support programme

At various points during the first two years we considered how we could structure induction so that new members of staff, whatever their role or experience, would develop some understanding of the way we were working. Catherine worked with the creative learning team to structure a programme that would, we hoped, give people an overview of our approach. We decided that we wanted as many staff as possible involved in the delivery of the sessions so we invited staff from each school to participate in the delivery with her.

Each session used an art form as a starting point, alongside an aspect of curriculum development. So in the first session the focus was drama and key skills, the second music and multiple intelligence theory, the third dance and linking curriculum areas, and the fourth visual art and the voice of the child.

In 2005 we couldn't release so many people from school so reduced the number of people supporting the group to three. In 2006 budgets will be further reduced so Catherine will work with one person rather than two for each session.

Indications are that the sessions have generally helped develop understanding of the work we have been doing and where we are with it. But feedback suggests that it has not provided everyone with the support they need. The process does have its limitations: it is impossible to provide opportunities for participants to become familiar with all the units they might work on in a year.

Teacher research

Teachers have been given opportunities to carry out research projects in their classes. They identified a question they would be interested in researching,

Ron, student on graduate teacher program

The induction sessions were great fun and it was also really nice to work with people you wouldn't normally see, people from Star. It was good to get not just teachers working with you but teaching assistants as well, having support staff to talk about a particular project really helped. Although I enjoyed it, it did not focus on units I would be doing later so, as much as I could see the relevance in a general sense, I couldn't see how at that moment it was keying into what I was doing. So as a general introduction into teaching differently it was very interesting but in terms of specifics there is nothing that will help me with the particular project I am planning now.

for example: How do I develop my pupils' questioning skills? Or: how can I engage a particular group of pupils more effectively? They identified a range of strategies for data collection: reviewing learning journals, polaroid and digital photography, video recordings, using dictaphones, discussions with the children and observations. They considered the value of each in revealing the information they might want.

Learning journals

One measure of whether CPD is effective is evidence of long term impact. A good example of this is the way children's learning journals have been embedded in learning and teaching and learning at various levels throughout the school. They enable the pupils to plan, record, evaluate and reflect on their learning processes. Learning journals have effectively captured the

Knowledge	Skills
Sewing and thinking a listening I have been listening to know how to do my stiching neat I'm not Perfect but I'm better than before but I hope I become Perfect.	Sewing has been Improved the most for me. and listening and co-operating and being helpful with the only boy in our group.

Understanding	Attitude
I understood my coo-operation with my group and understood why we had so many arguments because we wanted to get the Job done.	my attitude is fine so I think I don't have a bad Attitude.

Year 5 learning journal page

Lizzy, teacher

The teacher research helped me to evaluate different strategies for raising pupils' self-esteem. It also helped me develop my own teaching style and make it more interesting and focused. Also listening to what other teachers had done and what they had found was really helpful because they focused on different areas, their ideas also informed my practice. It was pleasing and satisfying to reflect back on the achievements of the pupils.

voices of the children and incorporated Assessment for Learning in lessons, giving the pupils ownership and opportunities for self-assessment. Using journals has proved very successful: teachers use them in all subjects and they reveal the transfer of skills for both the teachers and the pupils. When used well, pupils have gained insight into their own learning processes and their ability to articulate them has improved.

Evaluations of all professional development opportunities over the last four years

The level of staff satisfaction with professional development opportunities has been very good overall. Most staff feel that they have furthered their understanding of the relationship between the arts and learning. The interactive sessions were especially appreciated. Staff found them stimulating and felt they had a positive impact on learning and teaching in the classroom as well as on their own personal development.

Points to be considered are

- How can we keep the freshness and excitement of units we have developed over the years?
- Is the model we are using, which asks staff to identify their needs, still working for everyone on the staff?
- Are new staff receiving the right level of input during their induction or should we be trying to differentiate more accurately?

Catherine, teacher-artist

Stephen, our resident dancer, was instrumental in helping us develop ideas about how learning journals can be used effectively. We are still working on identifying a range of strategies which can be used to support pupils in reflecting on their learning.

The role of the teacher-artist – *Teri N'Guessan*

At the beginning of the project, the steering group agreed to appoint a teacher-artist to support the development of the project. Whilst both schools had staff with various levels of expertise in the arts, neither had someone whose work could be extended to manage the day-to-day running of units of work as we developed them. We also needed someone who was external to the schools, to take a lead in evaluation of the whole initiative. For the first two years, her line manager was the EAZ director rather than the head-teachers. This enabled her to build strong independent relationships with staff, children, parents and governors across the two schools, in a way that no member of school staff could have done. Her initial brief was to:

- support planning
- provide workshops for staff
- support teaching
- act as a broker and facilitator in establishing partnerships with external organisations.

From the outset, however, Catherine McGill has played a major role in the strategic development of creative learning. She combines the insight of an experienced teacher and art co-ordinator with that of a practicing visual artist. Working with teachers from both schools, she developed a framework for planning that incorporated multiple intelligences, key skills, learning skills and arts skills. She managed and led professional development for creative learning, ensuring that the overall plan incorporated the outcomes of staff self-evaluation, priorities in the schools' development plans and the skills and understanding required to develop specific art forms across both schools. This has generated a framework that provides differentiated opportunities for all teaching and classroom based support staff. She has contributed to the development of greater understanding of arts processes and learning across the arts through a combination of joint planning, workshops, partnership teaching and support for individual teachers and teaching assistants.

Her role has developed and changed over time, in line with the changing roles of leaders and other staff in the schools. As staff have become more skilled and confident, they need less support for their planning and teaching. Arts leaders and individual teachers now have more responsibility for brokering partnerships and supporting planning and teaching. Our long term aim was to become less dependent on Catherine as a catalyst for our work. We are succeeding in achieving this and are now in a position where her services are brokered to other schools.

Andi, writing in A+ 5 Years On

A teacher from Manor School accepted the position of teacher-artist and was appointed for September 2002. As part of her induction into an advisory teacher role, she continues to work collaboratively with and has received mentor support and guidance from the local authority's Art Advisor.

Over the first year of creative learning, she developed strong working relationships across all phases in both schools. She has become Operational Manager of creative learning at school level – through her presence she has been able to keep it alive and developing.

On a more strategic level, Catherine has jointly planned, implemented, monitored and evaluated teaching units across all phases in both schools. This has enabled teachers and support staff to build on their successes, asses their strengths and areas for development and consolidate their knowledge and understanding of creative learning into the next phase of their teaching and learning.

She has supported the schools in taking risks within the research parameters, by coordinating cross-school arts events and delivering and evaluating school-based inter school Continuing Professional Development.

Catherine had made significant contributions to the discourse on learning through her own MA research. She continues, through her own practice, to build a significant data base of evidence of effective practice that has been used to strategically inform the direction and focus of other EAZ Excellence in Cities partnerships of schools. As a key member of the creative learning steering group, she has contributed to the national debate on creativity and learning at the National College for School Leadership and at the Department for Education and Skills Innovations Unit.

Conclusion

We have tried to ensure that continuing professional development supports the development of creative learning and promotes the learning of adults across the schools. It has changed in structure over the years, becoming more differentiated and more closely linked to needs analysis for and by individuals. We try to maintain a balance between responding to individual needs and challenging thinking and understanding. Whenever appropriate, we make use of staff expertise and try to ensure that the experiences they provide reflect our beliefs about learning.

6

ASSESSING LEARNING
'Sometimes it's hard because you
know what you enjoy but you don't
know what you've learnt – but actually
you have learnt something'

This chapter, which opens with the words of a Year 3 pupil, describes how assessment procedures were changed to meet the needs of a changing curriculum. It includes writing by Kate McGee, deputy head and assessment co-ordinator and by Stephen Mason, dancer in residence, whose work on learning journals helped us to explore new ways of working.

Looking at learning – *Kate McGee*
We had reformed the curriculum to take three strands into account: key skills, National Curriculum skills and arts skills. This left us with systems for assessment which didn't fully take into account many of the aspects of learning we considered to be important. Our task for the third year of the partnership was to develop a system of assessment that took full account of our approach to learning and the curriculum.

Having embarked on creative learning, we encountered some difficulties in assessing subjects such as visual arts and dance. Our first task was to create a progression of skills for each of the arts subjects and each of the key skills. We

---

Teri, headteacher

We found the National Curriculum level descriptors very vague and they did not offer us an opportunity to asses the pupils clearly. Nether did they reflect some of the aspects we considered to be important in learning.

Expectations of questioning skills for Year 4 pupils
Pupils should be able to

> question peers' opinions
>
> brainstorm topics and come up with questions
>
> evaluate their questions and responses
>
> predict and give reasons for their answers
>
> use knowledge to enquire
>
> use questions to challenge a speaker
>
> begin using analytical questions
>
> give reasons for answers, based on prior knowledge

had much discussion around questions such as 'Where should Year 3 be in terms of painting?', 'What type of questioning should Year 1 be able to do?', 'What type of meta learning are Year 6 capable of? It raised the subject of benchmarks and comparisons of work. I led this process, in consultation with the staff; we were looking for information that would be useful to pass up to a new teacher, but also a manageable task for the current teacher – not too time-consuming.

Once we'd completed these schemes for each of the key skills and the arts skills, we had an assessment system that enabled us to track the progress of individual children as well as whole classes. These assessments are now done after units of work are completed, so providing a cumulative picture of a child or of a class.

Some issues have arisen which we are currently addressing. On a practical level, the high mobility rate among our pupils can distort the picture of a class, and needs to be allowed for when looking for trends over a period of time. It is worth trying to verify the picture you have built up about the class from the data. This ties in with the fact that staff are trying to acquire the habit of regularly using the assessment grids to update information, rather than leaving it to the end of the year. This means the information gathered can be more accurate. Ultimately it's less onerous for the teacher than trying to do it all in one go. I find it much easier to assess a unit that is just completed rather than trying to do it retrospectively – however, finding the time to do it in this way remains a challenge!

We have also introduced the planning for specific key skills into the weekly and session planners. This has been facilitated in several ways: by the

Barbara, teacher

Children have been given plenty of opportunities to evaluate their work and to share their evaluations with their peers. This has been highly valuable for their development as learners. The ability to evaluate their work has also progressed into the ability to evaluate their learning; in my view it's an amazing skill to acquire so young.

Learning from each other has been a fundamental step in my pupils' journey; one that has taken us beyond the boundaries of what is generally regarded as teaching and learning.

Kamilya, teacher trainee

Since working on the key skills, I am more inclined to let the children evaluate their work. I am much more aware of encouraging the children to think about the process of learning – this is reflected in all my teaching

teacher-artist and senior staff working with individual year groups, as well as through staff meetings at which it is decided how this might be done most effectively, and to ensure that the process is embedded into the planning. It enables staff then to have specific skills to teach to children over the course of a week, a unit or a half term. Specifying on plans which key skill I am focusing on has really helped me to be more explicit with the children, and I think it has helped the children to incorporate these skills into the learning process.

We have also been trying to streamline the transfer of this information to the next teacher. It can be used to inform the planning of another unit with the same class, or the same unit the following year, but this happens in a less structured way where the information needs to carry through to the next academic year. This assessment information can then be fed into the next unit of work, or passed up to the next teacher to provide a baseline from which to plan the next year's work.

Marion, headteacher

You can't disentangle teaching and learning from assessment. Assessment and learning are the same thing in the end. With every conversation you have with a child you are making judgements about their learning. The language you use helps the child move on with their learning. Some teachers see assessment as 'I must assess this child in Literacy'. They haven't yet seen assessment as day-to-day, embedded in what you say to the children. Creative learning has moved that on, particularly the emphasis on cross-curricular skills, particularly around questioning – that has significantly moved children's learning on. It's accelerated the work we've done around Assessment for Learning.

> *Leesa, teacher*
>
> There are more opportunities to celebrate the achievements of less academic pupils – great to let them lead a session or a group of children. Children are given more freedom to choose how to express their ideas – it was difficult to let go at first. Children have more responsibility for their learning – we guide them.

Together with the information about achievement and progress in terms of national curriculum levels, these assessments will provide a comprehensive set of information about each individual and a class or year group, year on year.

This is all summative assessment that in the main is carried out at the end of a unit of work or towards the end of the academic year. We also looked at and developed the systems for formative assessment that were being used in the classroom on a daily basis.

Self-assessment and peer assessment

Pupils have frequent opportunities to evaluate their own work and learning individually, in pairs and as a whole class. Ongoing evaluations are particularly valuable for identifying next steps and strategies that will support further learning.

Sharing across the schools has also had an impact on pupils' thinking about learning. They get to see the work of other pupils that may have come from the same starting point and involved the same process but has a completely different outcome. They learn to appreciate and value the work of others.

Learning journals

The ways in which learning journals are used has developed significantly over the past four years. They are used differently in different areas of the school, in the Foundation Stage and in Key Stage 1 they are teacher-led whereas throughout Key Stage 2 the children have started to develop a more personal and independent style of recording. The Foundation Stage often focuses on images, either photographs or children's drawings. As the pupils get older

> What's good with sharing is that you get to see how other people have done things differently and how you could have done things.
>
> *Year 4 pupil*

Conversation with Donna, nursery teacher and Razia, nursery nurse

Donna. We watched Stephen and we videoed it so that we could watch it back and see exactly what he did and how the children reacted. Then we incorporated that into our planning. The children laughed at it, they weren't watching themselves dancing – they were amazed that they were on television. This year we made a photo diary. We wanted to see which one was best and we have decided that video is best. You can't beat a video for watching dance. The photos are nice but you can't really tell what is going on in most of them. Whereas with the puppets the photos work really well.

Razia. When you are actually working out dances if you take a photo you can't always see what is happening because it's movement. You can't work out what animal they are pretending to be because you cannot see the movement only a shape.

---

their thinking and recording become more complex and can include different forms of writing and diagrams.

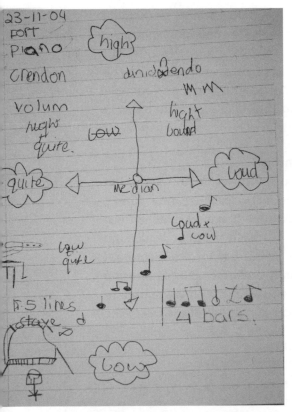

Year 6 Learning journal page

At first I found it difficult to strike the right balance between providing enough structure and allowing each child the flexibility to work in the way they wanted to. I found some children were initially quite nervous about having less structure than they were used to. The first time we used learning journals, I ended up doing more 'teaching' than I expected. It would be easy to make the mistake of just expecting the children to be able to use the learning journals, whereas in reality it is a skill that needs to be taught like any other. I had to go back and plan a progression of skills.

We identified that this was an issue across the schools and as a staff have begun to develop a progression of language used in evaluating. We are at the stage where they are being used in most classes across the school. Our task now is to create more continuity between classes, and specific progression in the way the children utilise them.

Michelle, teacher

I use more visual strategies, talk to children more about what they have learnt, use more discussion, getting pupils to talk about their learning, more continuous evaluation. I use learning journals as a space for pupils to put down their own thoughts on learning.

Sam, Lucy, Karen, teaching assistants

We do listen to pupils' views, thoughts, ideas and problems in them [learning journals]. Hopefully it shows that we value pupils' opinions

Monitoring how they are used can be time consuming, but does provide real insight into the children's understanding of what they have learned and how they can evaluate their own learning and prioritise what needs to be done next.

We have seen improvements over the time the children have been using learning journals. Practise has improved their skills! The children's increased confidence and ability to talk clearly about their own learning is obvious right across the school – as is their knowledge about their own learning. The children can identify the links made across curriculum areas, and can talk about ways in which working in an art form can enable them to learn in another curriculum subject.

Teachers observing teaching and learning

Teachers and support staff observe for various purposes in all schools. Because we had changed so much about our approach to teaching and learning, we needed a framework for observation that more precisely matched our model for learning. We began developing it as the two senior leadership teams working across the two schools. The initial draft of our classroom observation schedule was not at all user-friendly, and it needed customising to fit our situation. As a staff we developed a checklist that could be used to assess the quality of learning going on in a classroom. We started with the

Violet, teacher (on learning journals)

Children are reflecting on their learning in different ways...looking at the process and not just concentrating on the end product.

> *Teri, headteacher*
>
> We had a rough framework for observing learning and started piloting a set of questions around learning but we weren't happy with it. We had a small number of teachers try it out but it was unwieldy. The idea was that, prior to observations, people would focus on a specific number of questions. The questions we developed through A+ are quite precise, but we weren't sure we were asking the right ones.

question 'What would we see in a classroom where the learning going on was excellent?' The answers cover a wide area.

Teachers doing termly peer observations now use this checklist. In year groups teachers agree on an area of the children's learning to focus on. It might be an aspect of meta-learning such as 'the children able to identify transferred skills' or of presenting or recording learning, such as 'children are able to make appropriate decisions about ways in which their learning is presented'. After each of the classes is observed, the teachers discuss what they saw and feed their conclusions into further planning. We want to extend this system to enable teachers to do peer observations with staff in other year groups and to include support staff.

The impact of this focused approach to observations has reinforced the idea that what we are looking for is all about the children's learning. Every observation is looking at the impact of the teaching on the learning going on in the classroom and provides a forum for all staff to discuss ways in which that experience can be improved. The feedback from staff about this procedure has been positive; people welcome the opportunity to have such discussions with a peer, and can give specific examples of how they have consequently changed what went on in the classroom.

> *Teacher*
>
> I will make sure the children know how the lesson relates to the topic as a whole
>
> *Teacher*
>
> I learnt I should give the children the opportunity to explain their choices when giving them freedom and choice about how they present or record.

OBSERVABLE FEATURES

1: CROSS CURRICULAR SKILLS

a. children are learning to ask purposeful, reflective questions of varied kinds
b. children make links between curriculum areas, similar skills/ideas
c. teacher makes explicit links between curriculum areas, similar skills/ideas
d. children are learning to speak clearly and confidently, and listen actively to others
e. children are learning to make decisions and to express ideas and opinions

2: ACTIVE LEARNING APPROACHES

a. children know the purpose of learning activities
b. children show appropriate independence (choice of learning strategy, accessing resources etc)
c. children sustain attentive listening, responding to what they have heard by making relevant comments, questions or actions
d. all adults promote appropriate independence in the pupils
e. learning activities are engaging and promote active learning (discussion, role-play, drama etc)

3: PRESENTING/RECORDING LEARNING

a. learning recorded appropriately when needed
b. children understand why they are recording
c. children are given opportunities to present learning in varied ways
d. children make appropriate decisions about ways in which their learning is presented

4. PLANNING

a. planning is a working document used flexibly to enhance learning
b. learning processes are emphasised
c. assessment for learning is planned

5. LEARNING OBJECTIVES/QUESTIONS

a. children understand the learning objective
b. children are clear about the success criteria

6. META LEARNING

a. children can identify what they have learned
b. children can identify how they have learned
c. children demonstrate perseverance in a task
d. children are able to communicate their learning to others
e. children are able to identify transferred skills

7. ASSESSMENT FOR LEARNING

a. children reflect on and discuss their learning
b. children can give constructive feedback
c. children can respond to constructive feedback

8. APPLICATION

a. children are learning to apply skills / knowledge / understanding in different contexts

Creativity across the curriculum: Indicators of creative learning and Manor and Star

We might see children working individually and collaboratively

- showing creative attitudes of mind
- getting excited, smiling, becoming animated
- facilitating their own and others' learning
- recognising and working through frustration
- deferring judgement
- showing a mastery response i.e. learning is more about effort than enjoyment
- having aha moments
- doing nothing perceptible (reflecting)
- working at a level between excitement and fear
- challenging and developing beliefs
- connecting and applying learning
- showing independence
- learning co-operatively
- negotiating and discussing
- exploring, investigating, playing and experimenting with their own ideas

In teaching plans and practice we might see teams of teachers

- planning to ask questions not telling
- using fluid yet rigorous planning formats
- focusing on learning rather than activities
- creating time for assessment and evaluation of learning outcomes
- planning to use different art forms
- providing opportunities for children to raise their own questions
- planning for a variety of ways of learning
- planning for a range of teaching styles
- planning open-ended, exploratory activities
- emphasising process
- planning for less content
- sharing in teams but allowing for individuality
- ensuring structure but also fluidity (adapting during the learning)

In the school environment we might see

- children's questions and explanations displayed
- a range of outcomes supported by evidence of processes (learning journeys) across the whole curriculum
- parents fully aware and supportive of the ethos and engaged with the school
- classrooms that look like workshops
- children learning in a variety of ways, with quality tools and appropriate materials
- children involved in the process of display
- an atmosphere conducive to creativity – relaxed yet stimulating, challenging yet supportive
- children with access to a range of resources from which they can learn to choose
- strong statements of the essential elements of the vision

We might see school leaders

- stepping back
- allowing staff to challenge leadership
- tolerating and managing their own and others' uncertainty
- providing reassurance in the face of uncertainty when required
- attending to and allowing divergence and unexpected outcomes
- helping to create and sustain an overall shared vision but allowing divergence of approaches
- not being in charge
- learning alongside everyone else
- sharing knowledge
- celebrating the learning of others
- making use of in-house expertise
- challenging individuals
- building confidence by targeted feedback and support

Creativity across the curriculum: Indicators of creative learning and Manor and Star (contiuned)

We might see children working individually and collaboratively

- explaining and sharing their learning with a progression in the range and depth of articulation
- evaluating (self and peer) and giving/receiving constructive criticism
- questioning (progression in range and depth cf Bloom's Taxonomy)
- learning together across year groups and schools
- challenging views and opinions of others, including those in authority

In teaching plans and practice we might see teams of teachers

- ensuring planning is sound in terms of the school's shared philosophy of learning
- ensuring that children are engaged, having fun and learning
- encouraging and enabling children to articulate how they have learned and changed
- promoting two-way challenge between teacher and child
- listening to children's evaluations and using them to inform their own planning

In the school environment we might see

We might see school leaders

- modelling creative approaches and processes
- being open to transformation and cycles of change
- recognising that mistakes are part of learning
- learning from their own mistakes
- taking on board and encouraging divergent views and thinking styles
- creating an atmosphere of high challenge and low stress
- enabling other to find solutions for themselves

Questionnaires

It is vital that we know what the children think of the work they are doing and how effectively it is enabling them to learn. Since we began working in this way, we have used a questionnaire that all children in Key Stages 1 and 2 in both schools complete every year. The survey has two aspects: 'thinking about my learning' and 'thinking about creativity'.

In thinking about learning, we are trying to find out what subjects the children enjoy and which they feel they do well in, who they talk to about their learning, how they know their learning is going well, how they feel at the start of a topic, when they ask questions. We also ask them to describe a piece of learning that went well and why they think it did. We also ask which areas of the arts they like, whether they prefer starting or finishing, how they decide if they are happy with a piece of artwork, how they feel when they are doing art, music, dance or drama, whether they like to experiment or follow instructions. We also ask what they think they can learn from doing art, music, dance or drama, what they think artists are like and what skills you need to be an artist.

These questionnaires were initially administered by each class teacher with their class, but now the teacher-artist does them, to achieve consistency over the 25 classes that take part.

These surveys have provided a huge bank of information, which has thrown up many questions that have provided the basis of staff meetings and year group discussions. At a classroom level, they have given real insight into individual children's preferences and concerns as well as their strengths and engagement.

We have also used questionnaires for the pupils to evaluate each unit when completed. These provide an extra dimension in the evaluation and some-

Teri, headteacher

There has been a huge emphasis on [attainment in] Literacy, numeracy and science and that's what the existence of Standard Attainment Tests does. It only measures a very narrow bit of pupils' achievement... I think, looking at the kinds of things that are coming out of this work, the voice of the child is very much more useful in terms of what's happening with the children. There's a different kind of dialogue that goes on which is about learning. It's not just around literacy and numeracy. I hear it in the staff room all the time. There's a huge amount of talk about learning and it's not described in terms of levels but in terms of achievements in learning.

> **Amanda, teacher**
>
> I am encouraging pupils to think about their learning at a more conscious level. I am more willing , knowing it's ok, to allow pupils to express themselves in different kinds of ways.

times really surprise us. In the second year, in Year 6, I did a project combining literacy and ICT, in which the children wrote and produced a short film. It was extremely difficult to organise logistically, but I thought it was worth it. But the children were quite frustrated by how little time they felt they had for actually filming, and over half of the class were unimpressed with the finished product. As a result, we completely changed the way we organised that unit of work the following year.

Conversely, a unit of work involving maths and music that I found harder, was positively responded to by the children, both during the work and when reflecting on it at the end. My concerns were with the slightly less clear links and more open-ended tasks, which made it harder for me. The children were more in control of the direction and this empowered them.

Anecdotal

A lot of informal assessment is done through conversations: in the staffroom, with parents, listening in to children's conversations. There are many examples throughout this book of anecdotal assessment.

> Sometimes it's hard because you know what you enjoy but you don't know what you've learnt but actually you have learnt something. *Y3 child*

> *Emma, teacher*
>
> We now spend more time on thinking about our learning and questioning what we are doing. Children are given and take more responsibility for their learning.
>
> *Judith, teacher*
>
> The upside – moments when pupils said something that showed their understanding was deeper than I had imagined.

How do children think different forms of assessment help them?

The pupils discussed the different forms of assessment and made the following points about the different strategies:

Negative	Example	Positive
■ Testing, because if you just don't know [what you are doing well] but evaluation you can know more [about what you need to do]	Testing	■ It can only help if you know what you got right and wrong – then you know what you have to work on
■ I don't always like getting stickers because I think maybe next time I will get it wrong	Teacher encouragement: praise, stickers	■ I think when teachers say they are pleased, because the teacher is congratulating you for what is done ■ It tempts you to do your best
	Teacher marking: 3 star 1 wish marking symbols	■ I think teacher 3 stars and a wish because it is quite hard to do a self evaluation because you don't really know what you did but the teacher can tell you what you know ■ Teacher marking – it tells you what you are doing and what you need to improve
■ Self evaluation, because sometimes when you are by yourself you might not know something but if you have other people to help you and if they have other ideas that can help you ■ When you are evaluating yourself you might give a target that is easy to reach so you don't really improve that much ■ Because when you do it on your own you might not improve what you have done	Self evaluation	■ I can look at it and see what is right and wrong ■ I think the most useful one is self-evaluation because you can evaluate yourself and you will be able to get better at stuff like doing your handwriting properly
■ Sometimes people might not be your friends and they might say things that aren't true	Group evaluation	■ This is the most important because you get different opinions not just one person's opinions ■ Instead of having one person telling you what you have done there are five or six and you might find something that another person didn't find

How do children think different forms of assessment help them? (continued)

The pupils discussed the different forms of assessment and made the following points about the different strategies:

Example	Negative	Positive
Learning journals	■ Learning journals, because all of these even testing sometimes you get feedback about what you have done but learning journals you don't get feedback or there isn't enough time for the teacher to read it. Sometimes it's ok because it is what you think but sometimes it might be useful for teachers to mark it so they know what you think of your work ■ You can remember stuff in them and you can memorise it but you have to write a lot in it and sometimes when I write a whole page or two my hand gets tired	■ Learning journals because you can go back and look at all the things you done in the past and it is more useful in life
Differentiation		■ I know my work is going well when I finish a piece of work and my teacher gives me another thing and it's harder ■ I know if the work stays easy I am not moving on but if it gets harder then I am and I have to work harder

Reflections on Key Skills (meta-learning) – *Stephen Mason*

I wanted to see how the dance sessions could support classroom-based sessions and how pupils could record experience-based learning and use it to support their knowledge and understanding. Pupils need to reflect so they can record and make sense of experience-based learning and doing so uses all their creative learning key skills:

> Reflection lies at the core of experience-based learning. Without it experiences may remain as experiences and the full potential for learning by the participant may not be realised. If ... reflective activity is absent from a programme of experience-based learning, serious questions can be raised concerning that programme's validity and claim to be based in experiential learning. (Pearson and Smith, 1985, p83)

Reflection is a process that can facilitate effective learning through experience: experience alone will not facilitate learning. Reflection enables pupils to enter into deep level learning and so apply knowledge and understanding to themselves. They thus retain concepts more effectively. Deep learning requires pupils to 'make connections and draw conclusions' (Brockbank and McGill, 1998, p36) – a creative learning key skill – linking different kinds of knowledge. Pupils who adopt the surface approach do not internalise knowledge but merely accumulate factual knowledge through memory, leaving it unrelated to other knowledge. Whilst a majority of the learning that occurs in at primary level comprises of the accumulation of factual knowledge it is important that pupils understand, embody and retain the knowledge: reflection helps this process. Throughout the dance sessions we asked the pupils to reflect on their work: for example, when selecting movements for a particular task, evaluating – describing, interpreting and identifying areas for improvement – a partner's dance or making an entry in their learning journal. Learning journals were initially piloted with dance sessions as a form of reflection and their use was then extended throughout the creative learning curriculum.

The term *learning journal* is problematic. Here it describes a multi-purpose document that is more than a diary and might include a variety of media – for example, drawings, diagrams, key vocabulary, written entries – that enable

I think it helped me because at the end of everything I couldn't really think that I had learnt a lot but when I looked back I saw I had improved a lot of things. *Year 6 child*

> It's been helpful because it's helped me with science and like if every time I look back at it I can remember what I did in dance. *Year 3 child*

pupils to explore their learning. Carnell and Lodge (2002) propose that the journal enables pupils in formal education to connect between the various aspects of their lives: this not only enhances their learning but also enables them to learn about how they learn in different contexts and to transfer this understanding between contexts:

> Connecting learning is about helping young people identify and make sense of their experiences across a number of different contexts. The advantages of connecting learning is that learners can extend their thinking, enrich their understanding in a more holistic way, develop their insights about themselves as learners and come to a better understanding of their own learning. (Carnell and Lodge, 2002, p92)

The learning journals were used in this way in the creative learning context, facilitating the development of all the key skills through the dance sessions.

The pupils created what we called ideas pages at the end of dance sessions. Invoking the visual artist's sketchbook and modelled by myself, pupils used a double page of their learning journal to record their learning from the session. Entries were free and did not have to be neat; pupils could independently select how they recorded information, using drawings or key words. All entries had to be labelled, using technical dance and subject specific vocabulary. This ensured that pupils made links between their dances and subject knowledge. Ideas pages provided a basis for further entries incorporating extended writing facilitated by the class teachers.

> In reflective diaries young people can focus on a particular lesson or task, connections between different activities, reactions to feedback, comments about changes to learning and so on. (Carnell and Lodge, 2002, p19)

Using the meta learning key skill, older pupils engaged in discussions about how they were learning and their preferred mode of learning and were en-

Tula, teacher

Working with Stephen allowed us to broaden our performance skills. Not only was the work cross curricular but we explored evaluating with children in a number of ways.

couraged to add this information to their ideas pages. In discussion, pupils identified ways they had been learning about a topic during a unit of work – for example: listening, improvising movements, creating or performing dances, writing, watching a video, discussing – and declared their preferred learning style. Some pupils found it difficult to identify how they had been learning or their preferred learning style when the dance sessions did not overlap clearly with classroom-based sessions, but the children who could assisted them in discussions and helped them add their thoughts to their ideas pages.

Year 2

Year 2

The ideas pages became collages of pupil's learning supporting their ability to make links. But we realised that that this strategy might not be clear or structured enough for all pupils. After piloting the ideas pages we created worksheets with specific activities for pupils to complete to ensure that the reflective activities were clear and explicit, for example:

- draw, label and describe the shapes and emotions you performed to show how a *bully* or a *victim of bullying* may feel
- draw, label and describe what a *witness to a situation of bullying* can do to help resolve the situation
- Did you achieve your target for improvement this week? If so how? If not why?
- What do you think you did well today?
- your target for improvement for next week is:

Responses from pupils using worksheets were more focused, requiring reflection about their subject learning as well as providing opportunities for personal reflection. We referred to worksheet activities during later sessions and used them again as a basis for extended writing and class discussions. Class teachers requested that we provide examples on the worksheets as well as the sample entries of completed worksheets. Although this enabled the less able pupils to access the task, it led to prescribed responses or pupils copying our examples instead of taking responsibility for reflecting upon their own learning.

Working with Key Stage 1 during the spring term, the worksheets were created without sample entries. This required the pupils to be more creative in finding their own ways of recording their work. The activities were similar to the above and included:

- draw and label how you moved today
- describe what this picture shows
- What have you learned today?

We put key vocabulary down one side of the worksheet to help pupils label their work and make links. The pupils' responses were more varied and individual, requiring them to problem-solve ways of recording their learning. We used worksheets without examples for the rest of the residency when working with lower Key Stage 2, as they allowed pupils to make individual responses.

During the Year 3 Unit of Work class teachers were involved in the facilitation of the worksheets supporting pupils' ability to make links. Before giving her pupils the worksheets one teacher asked the pupils to think about how they could draw themselves *moving* and to sketch examples on whiteboards. The pupils' responses were varied and intriguing and pupils added to their pictures as necessary before completing their worksheets. The worksheets completed by Year 3 pupils were incorporated into information books that they created as a Literacy link within the unit of work. These books, created in small groups, were in effect group learning journals, incorporating a collage of science explorations, key vocabulary, discussions about learning and reflections on their dance work.

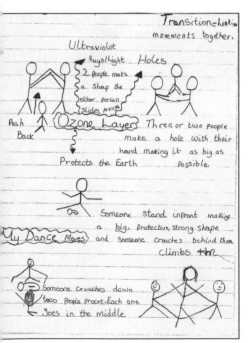

Year 5 sheet

The reflective activities described facilitate a process of discovery and exploration. They require pupils to analyse their work critically and make connections between different aspects of their learning. Moreover, these strategies can be used to form an understanding of the learning process itself. Not all reflection forms new outcomes: some consolidate existing ideas. But this is equally valuable in ensuring that pupils are making connections and retaining concepts. The reflective strategies underpin the development of pupils' learning journals.

Other reflective strategies used in the sessions included pupil and teacher discussions about their own and each others' work whilst devising and performing dances. Pupils were required to reflect whilst creating their work, by being asked questions. How can you make that movement clearer? Can you explain why you have selected that particular movement to represent the feeling of happiness?

Conclusions

These perspectives reflect a change in our focus, from teaching to learning. The development of a progression in key skills, with an emphasis on those that enhance learning in the widest sense, has led us to explore what we describe as 'deep learning'. Another key development we noted is the children's engagement in, and reflection on, their own learning. Starting as a process of collaborative pupil evaluation, it was widened to encompass learning journals and then extended to including meta-learning as a key skill. This process has influenced planning and teaching, as pupil surveys and questionnaires contribute to our evaluation of the effectiveness of our approach.

7

LEADERSHIP
Winning hearts and minds

In this chapter head teacher, Teri N'Guessan, explores some of the processes and issues that arose for leadership as the partnership developed. Hannah Williams, an arts co-coordinator, provides a different perspective on some of the issues and how they affected her, and Teri considers how the process affected her own learning.

Leadership challenges – *Teri N'Guessan*
Establishing an effective working partnership

We started out without any real rules about how the partnership between the two schools would work. There was clarity over how year groups would work together and about how CPD would be organised but our ideas on how leadership would be handled were only clearly articulated when Marion and I were asked to do a presentation for other headteachers who were about to embark on partnerships. After only a few month's experience of our own partnership, we had become 'experts'! We tried to analyse what had happened so far and came up with a fairly simple framework to describe how it works.

We decided that some essential elements for this kind of partnership are:

equality of status – this was not a situation we had encountered before. For both of us, most previous partnerships had entailed a 'strong' school supporting a 'weaker' one

being realistic about our strengths (and weaknesses) and being able to build on them further and learn from each other. This works at an individual level as well as at an institutional one

flexibility – a willingness to accommodate, even apparently wild, ideas at an institutional and at a personal level *being open to taking risks* – and knowing what it is you are risking

honesty and openness – we've had some very direct and forthright conversations

total commitment – to developing a learning community that extended across both schools. Sometimes this means compromising on your own school agenda

tenacity of purpose – holding onto the central belief that the partnerships can work

We identified and tried to describe some of the tensions that existed in the partnership at the time. Some of these arose out of the notion of collaboration between the two schools, others from embarking on a new way of working. Both of us were in schools that had rapidly improved in a very short time. In each school, this had led to tight cohesion amongst the staff and a great sense of pride in their school as an organisation. I believe that many felt somewhat threatened by starting work with another school. I sensed that this was borne out of feelings of vulnerability: maybe the other school is better than ours... maybe they think they're better than us... are we as good as we think we are? We saw some obvious competitiveness amongst some staff during the earliest joint meetings. Marion and I were pretty honest with each other about it, even though we were probably feeling just as vulnerable as everyone else, and we discussed strategies for dealing with the situation. We tried to anticipate where and when competitiveness might arise in joint meetings and made sure that key members of staff were present to manage the situation. We were fortunate to have excellent leaders with high levels of interpersonal skills –

Lisle, deputy head

Partnerships are tricky and they are difficult, whether it's between schools or the school and an outside organisation or artist. I think the underlying problem is that no matter how committed you are to the ideas or the ethos of the partnership you have your own agenda and no two schools are identical. I think that our two schools very broadly have the same agendas. We come from the same place. We have the same kind of catchments and are committed to the same kind of things but you always have your own agenda at the heart of what you are doing. When you are in a partnership and you are talking about what you are doing within that partnership, you always play through your mind 'How is this going to work in Star? How is it going to be managed? Is this the right thing for Star?' I think on a leadership level, no matter how much you are committed to a partnership, you need to be committed to your school first and that is where your priorities need to lie.

> *Andi, Sw Newham EAZ director*
>
> Another outcome which was not written in but came out was the schools retained their identities although they were working towards a common goal. They have adapted learning situations to suit the learning profile of the school. So there was differentiation within the programme.

this was certainly a job that neither she nor I, as headteachers, could have done on our own!

So on the one hand, starting a new partnership made people feel vulnerable, competitive, territorial; on the other hand, starting on a new initiative made them feel confident, interdependent, cohesive. That's a great deal to take on, at an emotional and intellectual level. This made it imperative to be sensitive to what each member of staff was experiencing. I struggled with that for 40 staff and worked hard to become a better listener. The structure of planning and CPD had an impact eventually. As year groups started working together more closely, there was more reason to focus on the collaborative aspects and to share expertise and experiences. Social contacts sprung up, including some very competitive football matches! These contributed to developing a greater sense of cohesion across staff at the two schools and provided an arena in which to play out some of the tensions.

Inevitably, closer working relationships were more readily established between some staff than others. Individual levels of commitment to the ideals and practice embedded in creative learning vary and so has understanding and interpretation. This is just part of the challenge; no one ever imagined it was going to be easy.

> *Marion, headteacher*
>
> The schools are very different and that is one of the strengths of the partnership, in terms of the way we approach things. But there's enough commonality for us to move forward together. We don't want the schools to be clones of each other. That's not the intention. The intention is, this is a learning partnership, so we learn from each other and we contribute different things.
>
> ... It works on different levels. I think there is a very strong partnership between Teri and myself and then there are some strong partnerships at year group level... but I wouldn't have said that every year group has that strong partnership. With some it's a working relationship because they have to...

At first our work relied heavily on partnerships with external agencies – mostly arts providers, as we needed to develop skills, understanding and expertise across the arts. Although there was significant expertise amongst the staff, we needed practitioners in the arts to support us and extend our range. This was easier when we had external funding for specific activities, for example the Education Action Zone funded the first two years of the teacher-artist; the Innovations Unit funded some aspects of professional development and a further two years of research; Creative Partnership funds helped us to employ a dancer in residence. Last year we managed without any of this. We jointly funded the teacher-artist's salary, paid individually for the musicians supporting us in Key Stage 2 and, at Manor, for a year long drama residency. This year money is even tighter but we have built into the basic budget allowances for all the arts activities. Some national initiatives have had a hugely negative impact – meeting the requirements of Planning, Preparation and Assessment (PPA) eats up so much of the staffing budget; restructuring has, cumulatively, cost a fortune. But I've resisted the easy option of using music or dance lessons as a way of releasing teachers. The staff need to be involved in the development of music across the school. How else will they know how to build on the children's experiences? How else would we be able to empower them to develop music teaching themselves? How else will teachers have the expertise and confidence to combine music creatively with other aspects of the curriculum?

In terms of funding, the way forward seems to be to make the most of free and low cost opportunities, as Michelle discussed earlier. We do this but are very discerning and far more entrepreneurial than we used to be. Catherine has approached arts organisations with suggestions about ways in which we could work together. She has negotiated with galleries the use of spaces where we can run our own workshops, led by school staff, so that children can explore techniques, materials and ideas arising from their current exhibitions. Some arts organisations have generously devoted time to listening and planning with us and have been involved in seeking funding so that they can provide support. These are partnerships where everyone learns – artists, teachers and children – and they are successful because they are collaborative and we learn together. We have also put in bids to various organisations to fund specific activities and are now in a better position to make the most of the expertise and knowledge we have within the schools and to tap into other local expertise.

Devolving leadership

Core Partners 2002 to 2004

Star Primary School	Manor Primary School
Newham Education Action Zone (EAZ)	Calouste Gulbenkian Society
LEA Advisory Service Art Advisor	Actorshop
Central School of Speech & Drama	Stratford Circus
Newham Music Academy	
and later Creative Partnership London East	

We started the A+ research phase with a formal structure. This was due partly to the nature of the research project and the high level of accountability for funding. The Core Partners (or Steering Group) comprised representatives from a range of interested organisations. Its principal role was to develop a sound basis for setting up and running of a two year research project. The formality was far removed from the realities of school. I found the early termly meetings quite daunting. In some respects, they were the antithesis of what we were trying to do at school level. They did, however, serve a useful purpose, apart from their principal role. Because we were working with a range of different organisations who were involved in differing aspects of education, the comments and questions they posed really challenged our thinking as school leaders and forced us to be very clear about the big issues.

The second layer of leadership was an operational group, consisting of the headteachers and deputies, the EAZ director and the teacher-artist. Martin, the researcher from Central School of Speech and Drama, also attended as an observer. The overlaps between the two groups posed some interesting challenges – principally in making sure that those of us in the Core group effectively disseminated information. Andi, who was then the assistant director of the Education Action Zone, was instrumental in this and played a major role in making sure that the two groups operated in tandem. Having someone external to the school undertaking this role ensured impartiality. At the beginning, I wasn't very aware of the need for disseminating the workings

Lisle, deputy head

People see leadership in different ways. I think there are some people who think that the heads, deputies and assistant heads make all the decisions. I think the steering group has been seen like that.

> In terms of vision and leadership, we can see in the reflections of the staff (at the joint senior leadership weekend) press for a flatter, more devolved, autonomous learning community... This move to more informed professional judgement and autonomy presents a challenge to school leaders; one which the school leaders themselves invited. But here we see evidence that ... moving to a learning community means a gradual re-appraisal of roles and responsibilities.
>
> *Martin Heaney, Interim Report, p44*

of these groups to all the staff. My perception was that we as a group were dealing with the necessary but rather tedious administration so we could create the time, space and freedom for everyone to work in new ways. What I hadn't realised was that many staff were under the impression that it was at this level at which decisions were being made.

The focus of these operational meetings was intended to be the implementation of activities across both schools. But we soon found ourselves drawn into deep philosophical debates about the nature of the arts, their role in primary education, the nature of learning and the relationship between creative teaching and creativity. We had embarked on what felt like a huge enterprise, only to realise that we were about to lead on things we didn't fully understand at a level that we could articulate to others. What soon became evident was that this debate needed to take place across both schools and at all levels. Without involving the whole of both school communities, the venture would fail. We had long discussions about how we might do this. I felt privileged to have the time and space to do this and felt that we needed to create the same opportunity for others. We also wanted to ensure that everyone understood their own leadership role in embedding creative learning.

That's when the idea of having a residential weekend for the senior leadership team came about. The plan was to follow this with the second phase, a joint inset day, a couple of weeks later.

What we planned to do with the leadership teams was risky for us as headteachers. Although we provided an element of input, we intended to leave the team alone and let them discuss what sort of leadership would be effective and how their roles would develop. It was a cathartic experience and one that, thankfully, proved very productive. I have no idea what was discussed – and have no desire to know – but the outcomes were wonderful! The leadership teams had obviously been critical – who wouldn't be with the opportunity to speak freely about their headteacher? However, they asked deep and crucial questions that set the stage for our next phase of development and, in my

Recommendations to head teachers

- step back
- allow staff to challenge leadership
- tolerate and manage your own and other's uncertainty
- help to create and sustain a shared overall vision but allow divergence of approaches
- learn alongside everyone else
- manage continuing professional development to challenge individuals
- make greater use of in-house expertise
- build confidence by giving targeted feedback and support
- model creative approaches and processes e.g. problem solving, leading meetings

Senior leaderships team Manor and Star

case, had far reaching implications for the direction of leadership. They produced a joint list of recommendations and a poster for each of us, with recommendations about how we should lead in the future so that we could enable people to be creative and be creative ourselves. I still have mine pinned above my desk, as a constant reminder of my shortcomings and my need to improve as a leader.

I realised then that much of the leadership had rested on the headteachers, teacher-artist and external partners. Much of the school-based leadership also hinged on headteachers, deputies and arts co-ordinators and this needed to change drastically. This was the starting point for some of my most significant learning as a headteacher.

The questions and issues raised during the Leadership Weekend led to a much wider debate right across the two schools. Members of the Leadership Teams (excluding the headteachers) facilitated discussion groups at the next joint inset day. It was structured so that everyone had chance to comment on everyone else's contribution. It felt just as risky as the weekend itself. Again the outcomes were thoughtful, penetrating and insightful. Again there was dissent and disagreement – it was real debate and it was taking place across both schools. The outcomes affected both schools as separate organisations, as well as our partnership. One of the most significant debates was around the tensions between creative learning and Standard Assessment Tests (SATs) in Years 2 and 6. This debate continues and, I suspect, may never be resolved.

These questions were raised by the leadership teams and formed the basis of further debate across the two schools

■ How far is the creative learning vision shared by all staff?

■ How do we convince people this is the right way?

■ Can we devolve leadership even more?

■ How central are the practices of art in individual creative learning projects?

■ How can we make people feel confident and take risks?

■ How do we support year group teams who are feeling negative going into the second year of the project?

■ How can we support teachers in doing creative learning units?

■ How do we help teachers believe that less is more?

■ What safeguards are there to ensure that people won't go too far?

■ What is given more emphasis: process or outcome?

■ Why are there varying views about the project, ranging from very positive to negative?

■ Do people really feel they can be flexible?

We thought that although the inset days had gone some way towards engaging people in the debate around learning, the discussions occasionally become bogged down in organisational issues. We wanted to provide a different quality of experience so we sought out a facilitator who would work with all staff in small groups, over a period of time, discussing their perspectives on creative learning. In the third year, a consultant, Peter Renshaw, spent five days working with the schools facilitating those discussions. He then collated the responses and grouped them into themes. Certain issues arose from those sessions but the issue of confidentiality made it tricky to deal with them in an open forum. Nevertheless we felt that providing time and space for individuals to explore and express their own views and understandings had considerable value. We wanted to offer another opportunity to the staff the following year, with a slightly different format. The introduction of planning, preparation and assessment time made that difficult to organise and only one of the schools has managed to do the second round.

The Creative Learning Team

Before visiting the Keynan Institute, the home of the original A+ Project, in November 2003, we started to discuss ways in which leadership of creative learning could be more devolved. We were particularly concerned that long

Matt, former deputy head

The dialogue is fundamental. I think the major significance of the learning-arts-creativity debate is that the very process of trying to define the terms and map the terrain is transformative in itself. In other words, the dialogue is almost more important than the outcome. I believe that schools are successful in promoting learning (which includes creativity) to the extent that the school community at all levels engages in learning related dialogue. I believe that the creative learning dialogue is powerful, especially because two usually distinct areas of discourse - the arts and pedagogy – are interacting. The tensions are creative, in that both discourses will, I believe, emerge changed and enriched. At all levels, teachers are engaging with what creativity means. The definition cannot be a top-down presentation but rather an interaction between classroom practice and theory.

Lizzy, teacher

I really learnt a lot from that, it helped me to focus again on why I do what I do and what I believe education is about.

term sustainability and embedding would only happen if leadership was devolved. We talked with one of the A+ Fellows in North Carolina and realised that we needed some sort of equivalent: someone who would 'champion' and model. To some extent, we had this with Catherine, our teacher-artist. But we realised that, to be effective, there needed to be a broader base. That's when we came up with the idea of a group of people, working across the two schools, who would fulfil this role. This was an idea that we returned to later, when we were looking for ways of ensuring sustainability after the end of the research project.

The formation of the Creative Learning Team took place at the beginning of 2004. We invited members of staff to apply through an open process – adverts in the staff rooms. We had no number limit in mind and recruited five or six

Marion, headteacher

The fact is that everyone is a leader and I want them to be the most effective leaders they can be. As a head, it's really easy to see yourself as the only leader. That's not good for the organisation. You can't invest all your expertise in one person or a small group of people. It's our responsibility to create leadership throughout the organisation – leaders for the future.

> *Leesa, teacher*
>
> It's good to have a forum where school staff can discuss ideas, give feedback or make suggestions to the management group. I think it's been particularly helpful when we have been planning Insets because we have different perspectives in the group and we all feel we can make contributions within the group.

members from each school who represented the range of staff who worked with the children from different Key Stages. The initial responsibilities we envisaged their taking on were:

- supporting others through discussion – clarifying ideas, planning and evaluation
- modelling good practice
- joint lesson analysis
- sharing understanding of different art forms
- undertaking joint planning and delivery of targeted Inset sessions on a range of issues.

As time progressed the role of the group has evolved to include:

- evaluating the impact of developments from their own perspectives
- raising issues
- providing feedback for the steering group or operational group on new proposals and developments
- school based support and advocacy
- embedding creative learning and supporting staff development

> *Andi, Director SW Newham EAZ*
>
> The way in which the schools have engaged in a dialogue on learning has a significant impact on the way in which children and staff view themselves as learners

> *Karen, teaching assistant*
>
> Other people know that I go to the creative learning team meetings so I can feed back any issues they might need to bring up. I feel more involved and informed. In the beginning we felt that support staff weren't involved that much but now we feel we have more of a voice and things do get changed as a result of these meetings. It gives us a place where we can say what we think.

These staff members have become a Think Tank which underpins the development of creative learning. The team also had a significant role in deciding on the nature and content of this book. Their activities have become even more crucial this year, as Catherine, our teacher-artist, has a larger workload in other schools.

My experience of the creative learning partnership
– Hannah Williams
The Creative Learning Partnership began in 2002. It was the start of a long journey in which the roles of educator and student would constantly swap, and all involved would be challenged beyond what they initially expected. What follows is a summary of my view, as an arts co-ordinator, on the process as a whole and a description of some of the issues that arose.

What was the Creative Learning Partnership?
The Creative Learning Partnership first emerged in people's consciousness as a way to push the boundaries of the existing model of teaching: traditional ideals were challenged and the true reason behind education was called into question. What are the truths in terms of what happens in a classroom? What do children take home with them when they leave? How much of it is really useful in their day to day life? Creative learning was, if you like, a call to arms for those who worked at the front line of education, and who were ready for something new. Working towards standardised tests was becoming too uninspiring; the literacy strategy and numeracy strategy had added structure and consistency but didn't allow much room for a high level of free thinking and real creativity within the curriculum.

The debate on creative learning called into question what we value as educators. Should we rather be emphasising skills that were more transferable, and encouraging a much broader way of thinking about life and the problems it will inevitably throw at you? Were we acknowledging that within a classroom we have thirty individuals who spend six hours of every day in a room with the same adults? Some of these children were still leaving school without the skills they needed to lead a successful life, so were we failing them? Maybe there was more we could be doing? Creative learning was diverging from the traditional focus of education and placing more value on skills that were not being taught effectively in most schools.

So, armed with paintbrushes, balls of clay, copious amounts of patience and some invaluable help, advice and expertise from all manner of people we embarked on a journey which is still unfolding and developing as I write.

Embedding the new curriculum successfully

Do we embed the curriculum, from the top down or bottom up? Part of what we did and continue to do well is keep everyone at every level informed. A small part of this responsibility rested on the art co-ordinator, but it mostly depends on the senior leadership team. People had to feel involved in the changes and ensuring that everyone was up to date with everything was challenging. If done inadequately, staff would feel as though the creative learning was something extra, an addition in schools saturated in initiatives, rather than as something meaningful which would grow from within the school community out of a recognised need to do things differently. How successfully could we embed this curriculum change and make sure it was a favourable transformation starting right from the fundamental level?

The degree to which these changes sat happily with teaching staff was the key to how successful creative learning would be. We hoped that it would become integral to our curriculum and daily practice, but this wouldn't happen overnight. I think that this was and perhaps still is a challenge. New teachers will join the school and their successful assimilation into creative learning will be another measure of its success. This would be one of the responsibilities I, as arts co-ordinator, would share with others. A happy teacher equates to a successfully taught lesson; conversely, an unhappy staff would mean unsuccessful dissemination of creative learning.

Practically, the project meant making changes to planning at all levels. Daily timetables would change, resources had to be ordered, people had to become confident about using the new resources, rooms had to be allocated, trips organised, extended planning meetings attended. This was all part of the challenge.

To help maintain the momentum and keep it meaningful, time had to be allocated for teacher evaluations. The next challenge was demonstrating to the staff how the issues raised, positive or negative, had been considered. This is not easy when large numbers of staff and children are involved – a problem compounded by deadlines and time limits. But the importance of making sure people feel listened to must not be underestimated. A school is a community in itself, and the success of the community is strongly linked to how

Teachers' evaluation

Trying to make links between different subject areas and cover all other subjects is difficult. Units take much longer than expected.

well we all accept that people will find different issues problematic and daunting and the support we offer. Where art is concerned, you have the added consideration that it awakens a lot of people's insecurities, often stemming from childhood. Who hasn't said, or heard someone say 'I'm rubbish at drawing' or 'I can't dance'?

The skills or qualities which I found to be most valuable were:

- flexibility
- open mindedness
- awareness of limitations (Teachers! Know your limits... and ask for help)
- identifying and accepting learning opportunities
- remaining positive
- commitment
- identifying and attach real value to skills learnt (what does this mean in practise?)
- being prepared to take risks
- being resourceful
- being creative

The changing role of the arts co-ordinator

We began to develop partnerships with all manner of people skilled in various art forms. This wasn't always easy. The art co-ordinator is the first point of contact for many people. I found that people often thought of me as some kind of all seeing and all knowing being. I learned to adapt to different needs and to be flexible with the resources I had.

As the art co-ordinator, I found it comforting to know that we were working as a partnership and that I was a cog in a much bigger machine. I was happy that the arts co-ordinator in our partner school was in the same situation and that we were often working on similar challenges and could support each other. I felt as though my own responsibilities had swollen overnight and the status of art had been suddenly elevated – I had to respond to these challenges. This forced me to ask myself whether I would have the skills to meet the demands that would be made of me. The schools had high expectations, a huge commitment, but at the same time nobody knew what it was going to involve and so it was going to evoke different responses at different times. It was unpredictable, especially at the beginning. This was exciting, and after the initial worry I began to look forward to all these new endeavours.

Tula, teacher and former arts co-ordinator

It was interesting to come from a different training base. When I first taught here (in England) I was shocked at how restricted the curriculum was for both children and adults. I found teaching to so many 'rules' strange. Hearing staff language and views change has been interesting to witness. I believe more staff are confident now to explore the curriculum in a fun way... not to mention interesting to teach.

One immediate issue was to start a dialogue between the two schools at the level of arts co-ordinator. I began to attend meetings with the heads and the senior teachers involved in the project. This was quite intimidating and took some adjusting to because, for a start, I didn't yet know how exactly I was going to be able to contribute. I think, in retrospect, the whole point of those meetings was to provide a forum for discussion and planning. One reason for the meetings was to decide the logistics of how we would move forward together as two schools. An example of the expectations of me arose when it was suggested that the schools should be involving everyone in making use of the galleries we have at our disposal in London and I was asked to take a key role in this and become one of the people who would lead others around the gallery and comment on a work of art – which I would choose. I found this rather daunting, but again, thinking about it now, I realise that I was developing skills that I would never have had an opportunity to had I not been involved in this project. Would I ever have imagined leading a group of teachers of varying experiences around one of Europe's major galleries? I think not!

This was one of the exciting opportunities afforded me as a result of creative learning. A lot of what I have learnt, apart from the obvious things, has been to do with self confidence. I think this is appropriate in light of the skills we began trying to develop alongside the arts. It wasn't just about the children learning. It was important that we adults absorbed these ideas as much as we expected the children to, and took them on board in our own lives as well as in our classroom practice.

Petra, teacher

Creative learning has given us greater ownership of the curriculum. Linking subjects in a relevant way has made the curriculum more purposeful and enabled us to spend more time enriching and extending learning. The emphasis on key skills and multiple intelligences makes the curriculum more relevant and encourages 'real' learning, rather than focusing on acquiring knowledge. The evolution of the planning process – from planning with Catherine to joint planning to teacher planning – has developed our planning skills and given us more control.

Learning as a leader – *Teri N'Guessan*

I suppose the most difficult thing for me, at the beginning, was trying to lead on a research project when I didn't know what the outcomes would be. It had taken over two years to move Manor Primary from the local authority's 'of concern' category to a position where Ofsted judged it a 'good school'. Faced with low attainment, low rates of progress, high staff turnover, high pupil mobility, poor attendance and a significant number of disaffected and disruptive pupils, using the arts to engage pupils in their own learning has been a remarkably successful strategy for turning the school around. I had deliberately recruited teachers who understood how this might work. I wanted a clear focus on developing an ethos that celebrated success in learning, individually and collaboratively. We used whole-school, arts focused activities to develop a sense of community and achievement, for instance, large collaborative visual arts installations, a dance performance in the playground involving the whole school.

The first two phases of A+ (the Education Action Zone project) had contributed to improved pupil attainment, quality of teaching and the ethos of the school. But as the rate of change and improvement was dangerously rapid, we were reaching a plateau. Each year, we struggled to compensate for gaps in previous learning and to raise attainment in a short space of time. It was exhausting. We needed strategies both to consolidate and to create a climate where improvement was part of the process of the school, rather than something we were constantly battling towards.

It appeared that we could not go much further within the frameworks of the Literacy and Numeracy strategies. To move further, we needed to go beyond them and to pay more attention to developing an approach that would encompass all aspects of the curriculum rather than focus on a narrow band. The ways in which we approached other subjects used the best aspects of the strategies, but were more stimulating and engaging – and were in some cases producing higher levels of attainment than we were achieving in the core subjects. This was particularly true of the arts. How could we combine the best of both?

I had initially 'used' the arts to engage pupils, hoping that this would flow over into other aspects of the curriculum. This had succeeded – but it raised questions for me about how we could really embed the arts, rather than using them as a vehicle. The emphasis on learning styles had demanded paying more attention to pupils' learning rather than to teachers' teaching. To embed this, we had to find more sophisticated ways of thinking about learning. It

Teri in interview with Martin Heaney, 2002

We've done all we can do conventionally. We've got some great teachers. We are happy with the curriculum – but we're still having difficulty engaging some of the children.The arts are a path to that because the outcomes are different. The traditional way doesn't necessarily apply…I question the values and emphasis in the National Curriculum – the societal value system behind it… we have to look at other ways of becoming 'literate' in the curriculum.

isn't enough to say 'This child is a physical learner' and cater for just one style. My belief is that people need to be able to learn different things in different ways – and to be aware that they do so and learn how to make choice accordingly.

Staff recruitment and retention improved quickly and dramatically. This was partly due to the level of challenge and the celebration of achievement. But it was essential to keep ensuring that the staff were given opportunities to create their own challenges and develop their expertise. We had a climate that encouraged risk taking but needed a more coherent context. While I was working on these issues, other ideas arose from within the QCA and Innovations Unit which emphasised creativity. We were invited to consultation meetings when *Creativity; Find It, Promote It* (2003) was being developed. Although impressed with some of what had been done, it reinforced my belief that replacing one scheme of work with another would not be a fruitful approach. Since the publication of *Excellence and Enjoyment* there has been a great deal of debate about risk taking but I have seen little discussion at a national level about how we can support people to do this. To a large extent, our approach addressed many of the issues arising from these documents but represents a move in a different direction. Whilst it can be very satisfying to feel ahead of the game, the challenge is to keep your feet on the ground and constantly question.

Throughout the whole partnership, I have found myself constantly questioning my values, beliefs and practices as a leader. At times this has left me feel-

Janet, former deputy head

… if we are going to commit to these kinds of things fully, we have a responsibility to support and train each other and the children. That's to do with being a safe risk taker. Staff have to feel the right kind of support is there. There has to be a range of support and learning strategies.

ing vulnerable, sometimes inadequate, but often coming back to my conviction that being honest and open was the only way forward. I remember the first joint staff inset days. I spent a huge amount of time preparing a presentation with the aim of convincing the staff from two schools that it would be a great idea to work together for two years. I had some persuasive arguments and a carefully structured series of slides, designed to demonstrate the great advantages this would bring. The night before the presentation, I ditched it all and thought more carefully about what was involved at an emotional level. What would motivate a teacher or teaching assistant to abandon working in established ways? What did it feel like? I thought I should model risk taking in what I did. My actual presentation aimed to do that – just an appeal to take a risk. I talked about the notion of taking risks, of how it was like jumping off a cliff, of what sort of support might be helpful as you jumped off, what teaching creatively might feel like, what might happen for the children. I talked about how I felt when I tried out new things and how I tried to cope with learning as a leader.

One of the things I wanted to create in the school was a climate of psychological safety. I wasn't sure how to get there or what it might look like but I knew it was essential for taking risks. I am a high risk taker but I also spend a lot of time thinking about what I do. I think learning is a risk: in order to learn you have to take risks. I'm talking about deep learning, for adults and children, where people are in a situation where they have to challenge what they are presently doing. Before you can move forward, you have to accept that what you are already doing is not as good as it could be. The fact that it's an infinite road makes it really hard. I believe that people have to be psychologically prepared to take risks in order to learn. So I sat down and wrote a list of what I thought psychological safety was all about. That formed part of my personal action plan for development.

Although there was nothing in the original research proposal that suggested that this process would have impact on leadership within and across the schools, I consider it one of the most far reaching consequences. The outcomes of the Leadership Weekend were a turning point for me. What we did that weekend was to open Pandora's Box. All nature of stuff came flying out. Most of it felt very productive and positive in supporting creative learning, but there were also some negative issues. It took me a long time to realise that this, too, was productive. It seems perverse, but the ability to cope with and accommodate dissenting views has been a crucial part of developing a more creative climate in our school. A debate can't take place unless people's views differ. At a human level, the most common response is to try to convince others to come to a common view. To some extent this approach works – we end up singing from the same song-sheet. We have a shared vision of the school and work towards the same goals. This was my approach when I first joined the school: Manor was in need of strong leadership and direction. But what if, by doing it in a different way, things work better now? What if hearing and understanding another person's point of view is more important to our learning than reaching agreement? Would that result in a more fragmented school? Or is it what a learning community is all about? It has been a difficult and painful process and at times I felt as if I was deskilling myself.

I joined a newly formed Action Learning Set with headteachers from other local schools. That helped a great deal, as I came to understand how feelings of vulnerability and inadequacy are something that we just have to work through as leaders. Sometimes I wished I could put 'being headteacher' on hold for a while, so I had chance to sort out what the job was really about. It took me months of questioning and self doubt. I haven't reached any con-clusions yet – but I now know that it's about learning. I could have read that in a book – in fact I often have – but I would not have learned it. I am eternally grateful to the consultant who taught me some techniques for coming to an understanding of what motivated me as a leader and, at a deeper level, to access my own basic values and motives.

Now, it may well be that I would have gone through this process anyway, whether or not we had focused on creative learning. But I think it unlikely. I'd taken Open University courses on what was then called school management. I did the National Professional Qualification for Headteachers and (far earlier than supposed to) the Leadership Programme for Serving Headteachers. I was paired with a senior – and very able – management consultant, through the Partners in Leadership Programme. I was clear (I thought) about the leadership styles I used and these matched well with the perceptions of others in the school, as measured by 360 degrees reviews. What was different about this was being in a situation where I had to learn about myself as a leader at a personal level.

I started on the process of restructuring leadership across the school. This grew out of the realisation that the loose knit teams which had grown out of new ways of working were much more effective than the old model of one co-ordinator leading a curriculum area, and my belief that shared responsibility and the idea of teams involving a range of people with varied experiences might be more productive. It didn't work well at first. The National Workforce remodelling initiative offered an opportunity to make improvements. The

Creative Learning Team seems to be the most effective model for us at the moment. As it consists of people who have volunteered themselves, and has teaching assistants as well as teachers, it is more effective than artificially created teams. Now we are trying a similar approach, with staff in teams focused on broad aspects rather than narrow curriculum bands. I am part of that process, covering for the assistant head who is on maternity leave. This is giving me a different perspective again, and an opportunity to learn alongside other staff.

Conclusion

It is essential that all staff engage in the processes of change, take part in the debate and reflect on their learning in order to move on and maintain a healthy, questioning environment. It is also necessary for leaders to take risks in order to create the climate in which these things can happen. The roles of individuals within the schools have changed over the years, with individuals taking on more responsibility at a strategic level, supported by a team approach.

Conclusion
A celebration of creative learning

Writing a conclusion for this book has been a real challenge. In drawing together the themes that run through the contributors' thoughts and perspectives, we've tried to focus on what is both common and central. Most obvious is the fact that we are in a constant state of change and that this is largely, although not entirely, driven by forces across the communities of both schools. Several contributors speak or write about 'school reform' and we needed to unpick what this really means for us. The ideas are brought together in the diagram overleaf. We show how one change, – writing some units of work – led to another with, ultimately, an impact right across: the curriculum, planning, assessment, developing independent learners, professional development and devolved leadership. Underpinning and central to all these is a clear focus on learning. We didn't start out with this model; it came about through an evolutionary process – one that continues.

We wanted to develop an approach that would retain the integrity of individual disciplines and work in ways that would enable learning in one discipline to be enhanced by learning in another. We began by producing individual units of work, building this up over two years. But we didn't want to replace the QCA scheme with another – hence the development of a curriculum structure supported by a clear framework of skills for learning, subject disciplines and arts. Using this as a basis, teachers and support staff collaboratively draw up a plan for their year group. In theory, they could rewrite this each year – but this would be exhausting. In practice, teachers review the framework for their year, the previous planning, the profile and previous experience of their class and year group and then decide how to adapt or modify existing plans to suit their current circumstances. There is always the option to abandon previous planning and develop something new based on the curriculum framework. This approach gives us a curriculum that changes year on year but which builds on previous evaluations and assessment. The hope is that it therefore better supports learning.

The greater the structure and detail of the curriculum and the regulators on teaching approaches and methodology, the less accountable teachers are for pupils' learning. The reduction of teacher accountability is a consequence of transmission models of teaching: the freedom to make more choices about process and content places greater accountability on teachers. This is reflected in questions raised at our senior leaders' weekend (see Chapter 7) and in the rather tentative ways in which some staff and children approached creative learning in the first year. Before people can believe that there is the freedom to be creative and experimental, they need a safe environment, where risk taking is valued and supported. So support structures need to be in place. For us, these come from:

- a commonality of view about what we believe about learning
- collaborative planning and evaluation within a clear framework
- devolved decision making
- acceptance that we are all learning and that making mistakes is part of that process

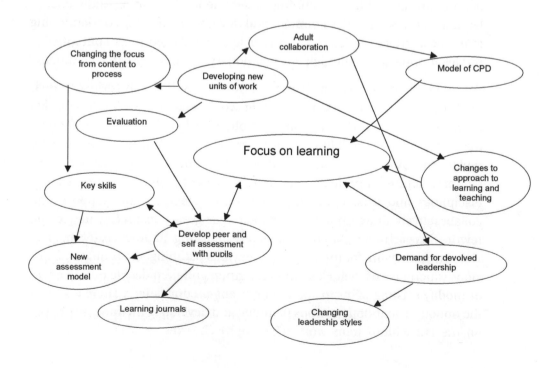

Although many of our staff are prepared to take risks within the structure, we know there are times when they find taking risks difficult. For example, in recent reviews in both schools, where teachers were observed by local authority inspectors, we saw a tendency to be less adventurous when being observed. We hope that if they have more practice and if we improve our support, we can help people to overcome this.

To a large extent, the success of partnerships is reliant on compatibility of philosophy and a clear structure within which partners can negotiate how they learn from each other. Our most successful partnerships, including that between the schools themselves, have been with others who have a solid framework and clear understanding of learning within their discipline, a commitment to maintaining the integrity of an art form, a capacity for analytical thinking and an acceptance of themselves as learners. Stephen's account of a three-way partnership – between children, a dancer and school staff – is an excellent example. Here all these elements were present and each member learnt from the other two.

One of the expectations of a book about creative learning is that it will tell others how to do it. This has not been our intent, as we are still trying to work out what it really means! One tool we find very useful for gauging where we are at as an organisation is a process we labelled Connecting Conversations. The focus is to continue a professional dialogue, across each school, involving all the adults directly involved in children's learning. Staff with different responsibilities meet in groups to discuss some of the big issues, facilitated by Peter Renshaw in his role of critical friend. The central questions for the discussions are negotiated beforehand, with input from the leadership group and consultation with the Creative Learning Team. We initially offered strict confidentiality because we wanted to try to ensure that staff could speak freely. The outcomes are papers, in which Peter summarises the discussions across all groups.

The outcome of the first round, in 2005, raised questions and issues that directly challenged senior leadership in the schools. We had indeed set ourselves up to be challenged, just as we had done at the Leadership Weekend. The responsibility of senior leaders for the process of embedding creative learning was questioned. This was difficult to address because of the conditions under which we had set up the whole process; our promise of confidentiality made it challenging for us to deal with some of the issues as directly as we wished to. We learned from this and worked differently the following year.

We end with the summary of most recent conversation at Manor School. We include this here because it is the closest we could come to describing the conditions that we believe any organisation needs to establish if they want to develop creative learning.

We can see from these points that change has come about but that although that change has the potential to be secure, it isn't yet. Five years ago we could have made a similar list after scouring research papers but it would have had less impact because it would not have been a lived experience. There are ways of working that allow people the freedom to follow their own ideas but at the same time reach a consensus; ways of working that have cohesion but allow for personal freedom. There is a clear parallel between the ways in which we are asking adults and pupils to work. They learn in a way that changes them – instead of transmission, there is transformation.

Manor Primary School Connecting Conversations
21/23 June 2006

Focus of this phase of Connecting Conversations

Building on the Conversations held last year, the focus of this second phase of discussions is twofold:

■ strengthening the quality of creative learning in the teachers, teaching assistants and children

■ developing a stronger sense of personal responsibility in the staff

Central questions

■ Identify a significant example of learning in your educational or teaching experience. In what ways has this changed you and your practice?

■ What do you consider to be the fundamental principles underlying creative forms of learning?

■ In what ways could you strengthen your responsibility towards your own learning and that of your pupils?

Principles underlying creative forms of learning

■ encouraging divergent, lateral, tangential thinking

■ exploring original and creative ways of solving problems

■ fostering imagination in different contexts

■ giving permission for children to get 'out of the box' and see things differently

■ facilitating dialogue that helps to shift perception and develop new ways of seeing

■ making links and seeing connections

■ exploring, sharing, extending and experimenting with ideas

■ enabling children to think about and reflect on their own learning

■ ensuring that children are at the centre of a reflective process that enables them to evaluate the outcomes of their work – exercising critical reflection

■ developing the skills of questioning and listening

■ engaging in learning processes that ask open questions such as why, how, what if, and what else?

■ challenging what might be perceived as 'right' or 'wrong' answers in a non-judgemental learning environment

■ encouraging children to verbalise what they are learning across the whole curriculum

■ building up the confidence of children so that they can take responsibility for their own learning

Manor Primary School Connecting Conversations (continued)
21/23 June 2006

Personal and collective responsibility towards creative learning
- sustaining creative learning throughout the school requires a shared commitment to both individual and collective responsibility: e.g.
  - senior leadership has responsibility for 'preparing the soil'
  - teachers and teaching assistants have responsibility for 'sowing, nurturing and growing'
- key aspects of fostering shared responsibility:
  - establishing and maintaining trust throughout the school
  - facilitating clear communication whereby individual staff take on active responsibility for finding out what is happening in the school e.g., regarding curriculum, structure, space, timetable, logistics, classes, children
  - strengthening opportunities for honest, open dialogue between staff, and with parents and children
  - encouraging the sharing of practice through peer learning and teamwork
  - understanding that responsibility for oneself and for the children is an essential condition for effective shared responsibility in the school
  - enabling all staff to develop an understanding of the bigger picture of the school
  - encouraging all staff to develop modes of evaluation that are embedded in a culture of shared reflective practice
  - providing opportunities for all staff to build up an ethos committed to creative learning
  - creating a supportive climate in which each member of staff is valued, individual voices are listened to and which actively promotes the practice of self-evaluation

Peter Renshaw, 30 June 2006

Glossary

Action Learning Set – a small group of people who work together to develop the skills of problem solving in order to solve work related problems in a structured and supportive way.

Artsmark – a national award scheme managed by Arts Council of England that recognises schools that have a high level of provision in the arts.

A+ – Arts Plus – an educational initiative in schools, originating in the Keenan Institute, North Carolina

A+ Fellows – advocates of A+ within the community of schools in North Carolina

Bloom's Taxonomy – descriptive framework of educational objectives ie knowledge, comprehension, application, analysis, synthesis and evaluation.

Calouste Gulbenkian Foundation – a foundation with a brief for funding and promoting programmes related to the arts, social welfare and education

CLT – Creative Learning Team – a forum where school staff discuss ideas, give feedback and make recommendations about the development and leadership of creative learning

CPD – Continuing Professional Development

Creative Partnerships – an Arts Council initiative intended to provide creative learning opportunities for artists and schools in deprived areas

EAZ – Education Action Zone

DfES – Department for Education and Skills

Discover – A unique space in Stratford where young children and their carers can create stories through play

Early Learning Goals – the targets for learning in the foundation stage

Excellence in Cities – The Excellence in Cities (EiC) programme was launched in September 1999 to raise standards and promote inclusion in inner cities and other urban areas

Guildhall Connect – the Guildhall CONNECT was designed to develop musical creativity among young people. It involves a large number of schools and community organisations in East London, and is innovative and imaginative in its approach to communal creativity, composition and the fusion encouraged between different musical cultures and experiences.

Innovations Unit – The DfES Innovation Unit acts as a catalyst for innovation and improvement in education. It creates opportunities for anyone who is involved with schools to work together on learning challenges facing the system, drawing on expertise within and beyond the education sector

Leadership Programme for Serving Headteachers – LPSH sits within the Advanced Leadership stage of the Leadership Development Framework. It is open to headteachers with at least three years' experience.

Meta learning – knowledge about ones own learning processes

Multiple Intelligences – a theory developed by Howard Gardner which proposes that there are a number of intelligences

National College of School Leadership – (NCSL) exists to help to make a difference to the lives and the life chances of children and young people through the development of world-class school leaders.

National Professional Qualification for Head Teachers – (NPQH) has been designed to prepare candidates for the rewarding role of headship.

Neighbourhood Renewal Fund – (NRF) aims to enable England's most deprived local authorities to improve services, narrowing the gap between deprived areas and the rest of the country.

Ofsted – Office for Standards in Education, the body who inspect and make judgements about the quality of schools and other provisions for child and young people

PPA – preparation, planning and assessment time

Partners in Leadership Programme – promotes the sharing of expertise between headteachers and business leaders and seeks to develop the management and leadership skills of both. Through developing each partner's personal skills, the programme works ultimately towards raising standards in schools and businesses alike.

Philosophy for Children – sometimes abbreviated to 'P4C' or 'P for C', is the title of a curriculum for 6 – 16 year olds developed by Professor Matthew Lipman and his associates at the institute for the Advancement of Philosophy for Children at Montclair State College, New Jersey.

QCA – Qualifications and Curriculum Authority

School Council Question Time – part of a developing initiative that is working towards establishing a Children's Parliament in Newham

Standing Advisory Council for Religious Education (SACRE) – Every Local Authority (LA) is required by law to have a SACRE. The responsibilities of SACRE are to advise the LA on all aspects of its provision for RE in its schools.

Transmission model of teaching – knowledge and skills are seen as carefully designed deconstructed objects which can be passed on directly to a learner

Wider Opportunities – grew out of the Government's pledge that, 'over time, every primary school child that wants to, should have the opportunity of learning a musical instrument.' The programme has had a significant impact on pupils' musical achievements and on their attainment and attitudes to learning across the curriculum.

Workforce Reform – changes to teachers' conditions of service

References

A + schools programme http://aplus-schools.uncq.edu

Andreae, G. (2001) *Giraffes can't Dance* UK, Orchard Books

Art Council of Great Britain (1993) *Guidance on Dance in education: Dance in Schools*. London: Arts Council of Great Britain

Brockbank, A. and McGill, I. (1998) *Facilitating reflective learning in higher education*. Buckingham: The Society for Research into Higher Education and Open University Press

Browne, A. (1997) *the Tunnell*. London: Walker Books

Calouste Gulbenkian Foundation (1982) *The Arts in Schools: principles, practice and provision*. London: Calouste Gulbenkian Foundation

Carnell, E. and Lodge, C. (2002) *Supporting effective learning*. London: Paul Chapman

Creative Learning Website www.creativelearning.newham.gov.uk

DfEE and QCA (1999) *National Curriculum: Handbook for primary teachers in England*. London: DfEE and QCA

DfES (2003) *Excellence and Enjoyment: A Strategy for Primary Schools*. London: DfEE

DfES (2003) *Creativity: Find it, Promote it*. London: DfES

DfES (1995-2004) *Professional and Career Development* http://www.teachernet.gov.uk/development

Gardner, H. (1993) *Frames of Mind*. London: Fontana Press

Golman, D. (1995) *Emotional Intelligence*. London: Bloomsbury

Hargreaves, D. (2003) *Education Epidemic: transforming secondary schools through innovation networks*. London: Demos

Heaney, M. and Shaw, P. (2004) A+ Final Report for the Gulbenkian Foundation: What are the effects of the implementation of the A+ Programme in Newham in relation to the arts, learning and the curriculum? (unpublished paper). London: South West Newham Education Action Zone. Available online at: http://www.creativelearning.newham.gov.uk/pages/publications.html

Hopkins, D. (2001) *School Improvement for Real*. London: Routledge Falmer

Lipman, M. (1988) *Philosophy goes to school*. USA: Temple University Press

McNaughton, C. (1997) *Here Coma the Aliens*. London: Walker Books

NACCCE (1998) *All Our Futures: Creativity, Culture and Education*. Suffolk: DfES

NTRP (2005) (National Teacher Research Panel) Research and Evidence Informed Practice in Schools: An Illustration and Discussion of the Key Issues. Available online at: http://www.standards.dfes.gov.uk/ntrp/ (Accessed 1 August 2006)

Office of Deputy Prime Minister (2004) *Index of England*. London: Stationery Office

Pearson, M. and Smith, D. (1985) Debriefing in experience-based learning. In Bound, D., Keogh, R. and Walker, D. (eds.) (1985) *Reflection: turning experience into learning* (pp69-84). London: Kogan Page

Smith-Autard, J.M. (2002) *The Art of Dance in Education (Second Edition)*. London: A&C Black

Sanders, D., Sharp, C., Eames, A. and Tomlinson, K. (2006) *Supporting Research-Engaged Schools: A Researcher's Role*. NESTA

Saunders, L. (2004) Evidence-led Professional Creativity: a perspective from the General Teaching Council for England. *Educational Action Research*, 12(1), 163-167

Simons, H., Kushner, S., Jones, K. and James, D. (2003) From evidence-based practice to practice-based evidence: the idea of situated generalisation. *Research Papers in Education*, 18(4), 347-364

The Place (2004) *Science~Physical*. London: The Place

Index

A+ North Carolina 73

Continuing Professional Development 4,
    3,16, 17, 54,55, 59, 75, 83, 124, 132, 134,
    141
Creative Learning Team 2, 127
creative learning units 6, 10-13, 14
curriculum
    development 8, 14, 90, 139
    planning   1, 5, 14, 48, 50, 56

Dance 8, 37, 41, 50, 61
Drama 42, 53

English as an additional language (EAL)
    34, 36
Excellence and Enjoyment ix, 134

funding 46, 122

galleries and museums 47, 51, 85, 88,

impact on teaching 5, 8, 30, 78. 129

learning journals *see pupils learning*
learning styles 43, 63, 69, 70, 85, 115, 133

key skills 20, 21, 38, 58, 62, 67, 100, 132
    meta learning 113, 114
    making links 116

monitoring teaching and learning 104
multiple intelligence 63
Music 37, 41, 44, 53, 91

originality 24

painting 19
partnerships 14, 45, 61, 119. 141
poetry 24, 26, 37
progression 21, 99
pupil learning 29, 30, 32, 38, 51, 57, 67, 69,
    71
    sharing 14, 15
    journals 16, 94, 102
    evaluation 65, 101, 102, 116

QCA 67

Religious Education 23, 28

Special educational needs 31, 33, 36, 49,
    69
school reform 74
self-expression 47, 27-8

teacher-artist 1, 3, 84, 96
teacher research 4, 72, 75
textiles 23, 91

voice of the child 17, 109, 111, 39
    questionnaires 18, 39, 109

workforce reform 136